DIZZEE RASCAL

TALES FROM DA CORNER

DIZZEE RASCAL

Alex Kitts

Copyright © Orion 2011

This edition first published in Great Britain in 2011 by
Orion Books
an imprint of the Orion Publishing Group Ltd
Orion House, 5 Upper St Martin's Lane,
London WC2H 9EA
An Hachette UK Company

1 3 5 7 9 10 8 6 4 2

A CIP catalogue record for this book is available
from the British Library.

ISBN: 978 1 409 1 33971

Printed in Great Britain by
CPI Mackays, Chatham, ME5 8TD

The Orion Publishing Group's policy is to use papers that
are natural, renewable and recyclable and made from wood
grown in sustainable forests. The logging and manufacturing
processes are expected to conform to the environmental
regulations of the country of origin.

Every effort has been made to fulfil requirements with
regard to reproducing copyright material. The author
and publisher will be glad to rectify any omissions
at the earliest opportunity.

www.orionbooks.co.uk

CONTENTS

List of illustrations   vii

Introduction   1

1 Mama Knows Best   5

2 A Problem for Anthony Blair   13

3 School Daze   21

4 Bow Selecta   29

5 Sound of the Underground   41

6 Off 2 Work   49

7 Dirtee Stank   59

8 *Boy in da Corner*   71

9 Grime Wave   81

10 Mercurial Rise   91

11 Coming to America 105

12 Showtime 115

13 Superstar 125

14 Under Pressure 139

15 Flex 155

16 Numbers & Words 165

17 Raskit Don't Give a Damn 183

18 Make Some Noise 195

19 Take Me to the Top 203

20 Strictly VIP 215

21 Living Large 'n' in Charge 229

22 Fix Up 239

LIST OF ILLUSTRATIONS

Photo of Dizzee Rascal, Netherlands, c.2000 (Photo by Collexxx – Lex van Rossen/Redferns)

Photo of Dizzee Rascal, January 01 2003 (Photo by Eva Edsjo/Redferns)

Photo of Dizzee Rascal, January 01 2003: (Photo by Eva Edsjo/Redferns)

Photo of Dizzee Rascal, June 01 2003 (Photo by Linda Nylind/Redferns)

Dizzie Rascal gestures as he arrives for the NME Awards 2004 at The Hammersmith Palais February 12, 2004 in London, England. The winners at the annual awards are decided by a poll by NME magazine readers, February 12 2004 (Photo by Dave Hogan/Getty Images)

Dizzee Rascal performs on stage during the second day of the 'The Prince's Trust Urban Music Festival' at Earls Court on May 9, 2004 in London. The two-day show was the UK's largest ever urban music event and was backed by the royal charity, May 09 2004 (Photo by Simon Frederick/Getty Images)

Dizzee Rascal performs at the Bristol Academy on November 2, 2004 in Bristol, England, Noevmeber 02 2004 (Photo by Matt Cardy/Getty Images)

Dizzie Rascal arrives at The MOJO Honours List 2005, the music magazine's second annual awards, at Porchester Hall on June 16, 2005 in London, England. The Honours List of 10 awards recognises 'career-long contributions to popular music', June 16 2005 (Photo by Jo Hale/Getty Images)

Hip-hop artist Dizzee Rascal performs on stage on the second day of the V Festival at Hylands Park on August 21, 2005 in Chelmsford, England, August 21 2005 (Photo by Louise Wilson/Getty Images)

Dizzee Rascal arrives at the MTV Australia Awards 2008 at the Australian Technology Park, Redfern on April 26, 2008 in Sydney, Australia. The event, the first in partnership with the Australian Recording Industry Association (ARIA), featured 8 musical performances and eleven awards presented across music, film, television and sport, April 26 2008 (Photo by Lisa Maree Williams/Getty Images)

Photo of Dizzee Rascal, Posed portrait of Dizzee Rascal backstage at Glastonbury Festival, June 27 2008 (Photo by Naki/Redferns)

Photo of Dizzee Rascal, Dizzee Rascal performing on stage

at the Glastonbury Festival, June 27 2008 (Photo by Naki/ Redferns)

Photo of VV Brown, Justin Timberlake and Dizzee Rascal attend William Rast at Selfridges on June 29, 2009 in London, England, June 29 2009 (Photo by Gareth Davies/ Getty Images)

Dizzee Rascal performs a sold out show at Manchester Apollo on October 7, 2009 in Manchester, England, October 07 2009 (Photo by Shirlaine Forrest/WireImage)

Florence Welch and Dizzee Rascal perform at The Brit Awards 2010 held at Earls Court on February 16, 2010 in London, England, February 16 2010, (Photo by Dave Hogan/Getty Images)

UK rapper Dizzee Rascal performs on the Pyramid stage at the Glastonbury festival near Pilton, Somerset on June 25, 2010. Celebrating it's 40th anniversary in 2010, the festival showcases some of the world's best artists from all areas of music and performance. This year's headline acts on the main stage include Muse, Gorillaz and Stevie Wonder. June 25 2010 (LEON NEAL/AFP/Getty Images)

INTRODUCTION

It's a steamy early July day in the hot summer of 2009. Everywhere you go London town is bubbling to Dizzee Rascal's infectious dance-floor-busting beats. A week ago, Dizzee was the highlight of a stellar Glastonbury Festival line-up, rubbing shoulders with musical greats such as Neil Young, Damon Albarn and Bruce Springsteen. The performance confirmed his arrival as Britain's first bona-fide hip-hop star. This week, Dizzee is onstage at Hyde Park's Wireless Festival, just a few miles from the council estate in Bow where he grew up. The 25,000-strong crowd from across the broad spectrum of UK music lovers greet the star as he bounces across the stage, spitting fast and furiously into his mic. Dizzee stops... breathes... looks out at the audience and gives out a big 'boooooooo' to his hometown audience. The crowd go bonkers.

Having worked the sun-kissed Hyde Park crowd into a frenzy with summertime hits such as 'Dance Wiv Me', 'Holiday' and 'Bonkers', Dizzee rounds up his show and hands over the stage to good friends Felix Buxton and Simon Ratcliffe – better known as Basement Jaxx – who are headlining the Wireless Festival that day.

Backstage, the mood among Dizzee's close-knit entourage of record-company employees, journalists and mates is jubilant. Drum and bass pioneer and good friend Goldie is with them, and everyone's in a celebratory mood, feeling the good-time summer vibe. As always, there's a bit of chirpsin' going on with the groupies who've flirted their way backstage. It's just another beautiful sunny day in the world of Dizzee Rascal.

Suddenly Dizzee's small crowd of post-show party people parts like the Red Sea to let through a posse of deliberately striding self-important men who purposefully make their way towards Dizzee. This is just the kind of thing that would have unnerved the rapper and his crew in his early days, when a post-show stand-off or tussle was a standard occurrence. A few security guys cock their eyebrows and mumble into their walkie-talkies, while those who remember Dizzee's early days bounce up and puff out their chests.

It's all a false alarm, though, as they recognise the young man who acts as if he owns the place (well he does, sort of). Everyone breathes easy as they recognise the flame-coloured hair and cherry cheeks of the man at the head of the crew bowling through the crowd towards Dizzee. Prince Harry and his entourage of mates and security arrive in a flurry of playful punching and comical street handshakes. Although Harry does almost overstep the mark with streetwise Dizzee.

'I never saw that one coming,' Dizzee later told the *Daily Telegraph*. 'Prince Harry came in and was joking around and being a bit cheeky, so I told him, "If you weren't royalty I'd have punched you in the face by now," and he seemed to like that. He's a naughty boy, so he fits in. In fact,' Dizzee mentions with his trademark cheeky grin, 'him and his mates are probably a bit wilder than us.'

Once the royal entourage have moved on, the singer Chrome – who supplies the vocals on Dizzee's number-one single 'Dance Wiv Me' – and rapper Smurfie – the most recent signing to Dizzee's independent record label, Dirtee Stank – laugh about their royal encounter.

'Did you see him pull those boxing moves on me, man?' Smurfie shakes his head in bewilderment at the familiarity of the prince and his mates. But Dizzee maintains that Harry and Wills could make it as rappers: 'They would rap about the trials and tribulations of being royalty. There's plenty of material there. They went to Eton, didn't they? So their English skills must be amazing. I reckon they could do it.'

Mixing with royalty, headlining Glastonbury, number-one hit after number-one hit. Dizzee's come a long way from his council estate in Bow…

1

MAMA KNOWS BEST

Dylan Kwabena Mills was born on 1 October 1985 to a Nigerian father and Ghanaian mother called Priscilla. Aged just two, young Dylan, as he was known then, was to tragically lose his father. He died suddenly in mysterious circumstances, of which Dizzee is still unaware today. 'There's obviously something that's gone on that's been kept from me,' Dizzee told the *Daily Telegraph* when asked about his father's death. 'But it's something that my mum don't like going into. It was hard to grow up not knowing, but I've got over it and just got on with life. And now I've built up enough of an identity for myself that I don't even need to pursue it any more… It's easy to get confused about things as a kid,' he continues, 'especially as all I really knew was that he died when I was two and I didn't have any memories of him… but the older I get, the more I love and respect my mum for how she managed to raise me up and carry me through.'

Dizzee went on to acknowledge that it was hard on both him and his mother, growing up without his father. 'I don't have any memories of him at all,' Dizzee quietly told the *Observer*. 'It was definitely difficult when I was young – you play the cards you're dealt, but obviously something like that can shape the choices you make in life.'

With Dizzee's mother never keen to speak about his father, the little he knows about his dad comes from other members of his family. 'It would be more my auntie, rather than my mum, who would tell me stuff about him,' Dizzee told the *Scotsman*. 'Did I miss his influence? Maybe, but on that estate I was hardly alone in not having a dad around.'

Trying to bring up a son on her own in the depths of Bow's rough East End neighbourhood was no easy task. The area is a concrete jungle of council tower blocks that are renowned for crime and poverty. It was a desperate place to grow up, but out of despair and urban dilapidation came one of London's most defining forms of music – grime.

Bow was the breeding ground for grime-scene pioneers Roll Deep, Wiley, Tinchy Stryder and Dizzee, all of whom grew up on its hardy estates. The area has since smartened up considerably, but back then the litter-filled streets were a maze of tower blocks and fried chicken takeaways.

Dizzee and his mum didn't have much, but even in those early days he admitted that one of his first memories involved stardom, telling *Wonderland* magazine: 'I remember I used to always look for myself on the TV. I didn't understand how TV worked. When a programme was on, I'd be thinking, "Where am I?" and looking for myself. I never saw myself.' Perhaps he was a prophetic child, because in a couple of decades he wouldn't be able to turn on the TV without seeing himself.

Dizzee lived on the decaying Crossways Estate on Devons Road (also known as the Devons Estate), which was built in the seventies and comprises one low-rise block and three tower blocks looming twenty-five storeys high over the local area, providing a total of 298 homes. The development sprawls out of a former railway cutting below the level of the surrounding streets and the towers are reached by a series of access bridges. The estate is famous for its poor condition and is said to be extremely unpopular with existing and prospective residents.

For Dizzee and his mum the bridges and walkways that criss-cross between the towers were the sole means of getting around the estate. There were open green spaces below the bridges, but they were permanently occupied by gangs and robberies and assault were common, so as a young boy Dizzee would have been told to avoid them.

Most of the flats on Dizzee's estate were three-bedroom family-sized units, including those on the higher floors. Suicide by jumping off the roof or out of the higher-floor windows was not unheard of. Overcrowding was, and still is, a common issue, with large families of up to a dozen routinely squeezing into each flat. While there is a nucleus of long-standing residents, over 40 per cent of the rental flats in the tower blocks are either void or let as temporary placements by homeless services because many people refuse to live in such squalid conditions.

There were constant promises to regenerate the area, but while Dizzee was there he saw little improvement. Looking back on his time in Bow he has a lot of bad memories, but despite all that he still claims to be proud of his roots, telling

NME in 2009, 'I'm not gonna lie; I don't always like everything about Bow and I don't always like everyone in Bow and they don't always like me, but on the whole I love where I come from. I'm proud of where I come from and I'm proud to represent that area.'

Dizzee grew up in one of the ground-floor, split-level council maisonettes in Holyhead Close. It was built over the Docklands Light Railway, and every three or four minutes, all day every day, he could hear City commuters zip past his flat and on to a better life. It was just Dizzee and his mum against the world. He knows that he wouldn't be where he is today if it weren't for the strong guiding hand of his mother, who had to play the roles of both father and mother as he grew up.

'My mum was full on, and she did the best she could – she beat me when she had to,' Dizzee recounts to the *Observer*. Dizzee's mum, Priscilla Mills, worked round the clock to provide for her only son and he remembers her hard-working attitude well, telling the *Observer*, 'All my childhood she was studying law to be a legal secretary, and any honest thing possible to make money she did – cleaning jobs, selling clothes, being an Avon lady. She worked and worked and worked to put food on the table and pay the childminder.'

While doing all this his mother used to try and steer him away from the violent street life that surrounded them. 'Looking back on it now there was a lot mess about it, it was rough and violent,' Dizzee told *The Student Pocket Guide*. 'I had to learn a lot of lessons early. I had a good mum, man; she did a lot for me. She showed me and she's a big part of how I look at life, just working hard no matter what. Do you know what, I never saw my mum sit there and just lay about and get benefits or nothing like that. Even when she was ill she would go to work, whenever she could she'd be working, working, working, three jobs if she had to.'

Priscilla's hard-working ethic, drive and determination rubbed off on Dizzee, who claims that she is his inspiration. 'She was the original hustler, a single parent in a council flat, whateva, but a real go-getter who never claimed benefits and always grafted,' Dizzee told the *Scotsman*. 'She used to sell clothes on the estate and I'd help... she packed envelopes, she cleaned – everything. That's where I get my entrepreneurial spirit from.'

Years later Dizzee would still remember all the trouble he put his mother through, naming it as one of his biggest regrets. When asked by the *Guardian*, 'To whom would you most like to say sorry, and why?' Dizzee replied, 'To my mum, for being such a fucker when I was little.' In the same interview he also remembers that it was his mother who gave him the worst job he's ever had. When he was asked: 'What is the worst job you've done?' Dizzee replied, 'Sealing envelopes. My mum made me do it. There were fifteen boxes – thousands of envelopes. We were up all night and I had to go to school the next morning. I hated it.'

With his mother out working all the time and without any brothers and sisters or father, Dizzee had a lonely, solitary childhood. 'I grew up and learnt to hold my own,' he recalled to the *Guardian*. 'My mum was doing two people's jobs. It makes you grow up early. There's less people to talk to, less close people, innit? You're going to end up being lonely because you think a bit more. I had to learn to be a man myself.'

Dizzee's mother came from a traditional Ghanaian town,

where family values, hard work and, most importantly, religion provided the framework for a healthy, happy life. Moving to the melting pot of manic London was a big change for her and she tried hard to pass on her honest, traditional values to Dizzee. This was done, especially, through bringing him to church. Dizzee regularly went with his mother to many of East London's black-led churches, where he was introduced to black music, in the form of gospel, through the church choir. Dizzee recalled to the *Daily Telegraph* that he and his mum went to 'all different types, but mainly the Pentecostal ones with a choir, like you see in America. Until I reached the age where I could say, "Nah, I'm not going", because it had been forced on me so much as a kid. Looking back now, though, I'm glad she made me go, because I think that's where my independence has come from, more than anything – from my mum and the Church.'

These days he doesn't go to church as much but he retains some of his Christian values and beliefs from his religious upbringing. Telling *The Times*, 'I was raised in the Church and, yeah, I pray sometimes. But I talk to God in my own way, and my own time.'

All the way through his troubled youth Dizzee had three constants – his mum, the streets and music – all of which helped him deal with his anger at the world. His mother tried to keep him off the streets by encouraging his musical passions. 'Even when I was getting kicked out of school I still made music. I found a way to channel my energies into being creative instead of destructive.' His mother recognised that music was a good escape for him and with the little money she had 'she bought my first turntable', Dizzee told the *Daily Mirror*.

But despite having his mother's love and encouragement with regard to music, he would still get into trouble out on the streets, particularly when it came to fighting. 'I was a violent kid for a start,' he tells the *Observer*. 'A lot of fighting. Probably I had to prove something. There was no man in my house, the classic story. It was quite a tough estate. Not the worst. But you needed to look after yourself from primary school on.'

Dizzee learned to look after himself the only way he knew, the street way, which of course led to crime and fighting. 'My life was just very violent. I grew up in a very violent area and in a very violent culture.' Dizzee told the *Sun*. 'It's all across London… there was a lot of fighting. There's nothing I regret. If anyone wanted a piece of me they had to be prepared for the revenge. I got arrested a lot. It was all juvenile stuff. It was nothing that's on my record any more. It's all in the past.'

Before Dizzee made it as a musician he indulged in a life of petty crime to help make ends meet, but he always knew that he was going to get out of the ghetto through music. 'Don't get me wrong, I made money from crime, but I never for one moment thought that was what I'd spend my life doing.' In spite of this, Dizzee still had the support of his mother, who helped him stay strong and realise that this wasn't the life for him. 'So when I had my little stint of doing illegal bullshit as a teenager, I wasn't proud. That's why I got out quick and did something honest instead.' But it took a few close encounters with violence, crime and the law before Dizzee learned his lesson…

2

A PROBLEM FOR
ANTHONY BLAIR

Dizzee was very much a child of the New Labour years, being just eleven in 1997 when Tony Blair became prime minister. Under the new prime minister's reign, Britain saw one of the biggest economic booms in history, but what that meant for Dizzee was that the country and the city around him got rich while the problems on the estate stayed the same. There was a lot of anger at the time, and violence and crime kicked off all around him. 'When you see what's going on around you, you kind of start taking part in it,' Dizzee explained in an interview with *The Student Pocket Guide*.

In 1998, Britain's new prime minister introduced the much-publicised Anti-Social Behaviour Order, or ASBO. Tony Blair and the New Labour government wanted to bring an end to low-level street crime and stop estate kids like Dizzee from being 'a public nuisance', as some politicians put it. But it must have felt like nobody understood or cared about his problems. Angered by what Dizzee and his mates saw as society turning on estate kids like himself, he rebelled and stuck two fingers up at the system.

'Basically I was part of the crime wave in my area,' Dizzee explained to *The Financial Times* some years later. 'They put up signs in train stations because of kids like me. I've still got friends that are going through some situations. I can never forget where I'm from.'

Dizzee's old neighbourhood, Bow, was notorious for crime, poverty and violence in the early noughties, but without this environment he would never have moved in the successful direction he took. 'Growing up there shaped me to an extent,' Dizzee told the *Independent*. 'It makes your outlook narrower – you've got less opportunity.' The lack of any real options frustrated him and his mates. Dizzee grew up surrounded by violence from a very young age. 'It's fucked,' he said of his old neighbourhood in an interview with *Blender*. Aged just ten years old he saw his first dead body, a man killed by his wife, and it wasn't long before anger and disillusionment pushed Dizzee into petty crime.

The police soon got to know who Dylan Mills was as he started getting a name for himself as a troublemaker on his local estate. 'When I was a bit older the police would be round the house. I had a bit of a temper on me so there was a lot of fighting,' Dizzee recalls.

In his early teens he bunked off school a lot and knocked about the estate where he saw some nasty stuff. Dizzee and his mates reacted to their tough surroundings by getting up to no good whenever possible. It was at about this time that petty crime became Dizzee's main hobby, alongside music. 'There were all sorts of temptations like thieving, drugs and fighting,' recalled Dizzee to the *Sun*. 'I once saw someone commit suicide. It's all standard for the inner city and I was into it all at first. I was conflicted and did things I'm not proud of. I knew I had to push myself if I wanted to make music. I didn't want the life of a criminal.'

It's a period in his life that Dizzee now looks back on as reckless and foolish. Not having a father figure to guide him had a big influence on his behaviour, Dizzee reckons: 'I fell into a lot of things that my mum told me not to do and there was no father figure to take me in hand.' Most of Dizzee's mates were in a similar situation and they used to encourage each other to steal and fight. 'It was stupid stuff,' Dizzee told the *Daily Mirror*. 'Joyriding, street crime, violent disorder. I was wild, but I wasn't an organised criminal. There's a degree of skill involved in it – there must be as I was never caught. I don't wanna justify it – it was like a phase. It's easy to copy what you see around you – it's all about peer pressure.'

As Dizzee and his mates got older the level of misbehaviour increased. They were bored and would get up to no good around the streets of East London for much of his early teens. Robbing cars and pizza delivery men were both favourite pastimes. 'I stole a few cars but it was just a phase I was going through,' Dizzee told *The Student Pocket Guide*. 'That pizza man thing, people talk like it was like a career. It wasn't a career, I just lived on the estate, and it was a normal thing. The pizza man would come and you just go and take the pizza innit – you know, out of the box on the bike.'

Dizzee's stint of doing 'illegal bullshit', as he called it, nearly ruined his dreams of becoming the superstar he is today. Feeling rejected by society, he found comfort in his local gang of mates, who knocked about the estates at night getting up to mischief and forming a family-like bond through their troublemaking. Society and politicians like to give what Dizzee was getting into a label like 'anti-social' and 'nuisance', but for Dizzee it was an escape from the restrictive reality of his surroundings.

Thankfully music would save Dizzee before things got any more serious, such as drugs and the problems that come with that scene. 'By the time my friends dabbled in the whole crack [cocaine] thing when we were sixteen or seventeen, I was making money from music. So that kind of let me be around them, but also to kick back and really see what the gangster life was about. The early mornings, maybe some of the kidnappings, the this, the that, the dropping offs, the crack dens, the crackheads coming out of nowhere, all the not-so-nice shit, the Feds putting guns to your head on the floor, random stoppings, all the bullshit. So I got to see that early.'

But even Dizzee's small-time level of crime would evolve into something more sinister. Gang culture and violence became a reality for Dizzee when he was only a young teenager as kids would start fights, often between rival estates and using nasty weapons. 'I've got friends that, when they were fourteen, fifteen, they got stabbed,' recalls Dizzee. The constant threat of violence turned his friends into a form of protection – something that was all the more important on the estates.

Without much of a family to speak of, Dizzee's gang became his surrogate siblings. The other estate kids all had similar backgrounds and were just as angry at their surroundings. 'That's what the gang thing is about,' Dizzee says. "Roaming about in packs of boys up to no good. A lot of those boys come from single-parent homes, just trying to find their way. It's misguided; that ain't how to be a man. You're just causing havoc, but at the time it's what you feel.' In *Boy in da Corner* he sums up his hopes for the future at this time: 'When we ain't kids no more will it still be about what it is right now? Bank scams, street robberies, shotters, blotters or HMP.'

In the late nineties gun violence started to kick off big time in and around London. So much so that the police launched an infamous initiative to fight gun crime in the capital called Operation Trident, which was aimed at bringing down murder rates and drug-related gun violence in black communities. Dizzee was an innocent bystander on the streets, but he still witnessed the ferocity of both sides of the war – from the police and from the street criminals.

'I ain't been short of people dying, getting shot and stabbed. That was always near me: fighting, bullshit, drugs, car crashes, crime.' Dizzee told the *Independent*. He was often given grief by the law personally, and he still feels like the troubles of the street can affect him, even if he's tough enough to handle it now. 'I still get the same bullshit that some black boys get. The police… whatever. The world's a jungle in my eyes, innit? Everything's tribal. If you see someone who don't look like you – especially the colour of your skin – you're going to be suspicious, or not as welcoming or warming, innit? I've learned not to take it too personal. Just don't fucking… don't cross the line with me. It'll be safer for everyone.'

In Bow during his early teens Dizzee saw more and more

people going down a dark route towards serious crime, but it wasn't just his neighbourhood. London was going down a rough road in the early years of the new Millennium. 'About two or three years ago', Dizzee told the *Guardian* a few years after leaving Bow, 'more and more people started getting shot; there were more guns about. Was it easy to get hold of a gun? It depends on who you are and how serious you are about getting them. It ain't just Bow or East London. Everybody knows there's a gun thing in this city.' As Dizzee says in *Boy in da Corner*, rival gangs used to settle disputes with their fists, now often they turned to their guns.

Dizzee looks back on those days with a mature head on his shoulders, and in hindsight he can only see how stupid and immature it all is. He can also see how lucky he was not to get sucked in. In the end Dizzee was too smart to lose his life to crime and violence: 'There's a big difference between being a naughty boy and a career criminal and I never graduated to becoming a career criminal,' he explains.

Luckily Dizzee saw the gang culture that was big on the streets of Bow as a waste of time, and realised early on that it wasn't something he wanted to be part of: 'I could never get my head around the whole gang thing,' he says. 'It was always a bunch of guys fighting with each other. There was a lot of backstabbing. I worked that out at fifteen and never got sucked in too deep.' These days he looks upon gang culture and violence as a symptom of male ego and guys not being able to communicate properly. 'A lot of the shit that goes on there is to do with communication,' he says. 'Young guys just don't know how to communicate. One look can make things go up in smoke, and before you know it people are in hospital.' These days Dizzee tries to disassociate himself from his chequered past and doesn't believe in glamorising it, like many other urban music artists do. 'Cause I'm trying to make music,' says Dizzee. 'A mistake with a lot of hip-hop is the bombardment of that stuff. I know other stuff as well.'

Dizzee has acknowledged that one of the best ways to avoid gang culture and street violence was through music, and he still preaches that to kids today. Dizzee feels that if wannabe musicians are serious about getting out of the ghetto and making a life for themselves they've got to give up crime and petty distractions and concentrate solely on music: 'Everything that you think you have got on the side line is just taking up space... If you're the kind of person who is focused and you've got that fire and that burn, you'll make a way in music. You'll find a way to get paid. If you're thinking about something else that is nothing to do with it, it takes as much mental space and time. It's conflicting. You're kind of fucking yourself up.'

3

SCHOOL DAZE

Dizzee had all the right tools to achieve highly at school. He was intelligent, confident and articulate (in his own street way), and he didn't struggle to grasp the skills and information his teachers were trying to pass on to him. He would do well in aptitude exams and should have got good grades, but his behaviour was always an issue. 'I was in the top classes,' Dizzee told the *Sun*. 'I was up there, but then my behaviour would slip – boredom, frustration and issues – so I shouted at the world.'

As a young and angry child, Dizzee didn't fit into the system and ended up getting expelled from four schools in four years! He was angry at the world because he didn't have a father, he was angry because his mother had to work so hard and he was angry because everywhere he looked he saw people in the same situation. He felt betrayed by the world and trapped, so he lashed out on the only system he knew: school and the authority that came with it.

'I definitely had a problem with authority,' Dizzee admits. 'I just remember feeling really suppressed at school. I think a lot of young black boys feel that way growing up. Whether it's being poor, and just not understanding, kind of, why you? Whatever the reason. You end up lashing out. There's so much that you take until eventually you just say, "Fuck it!"'

He got kicked out of school for being naughty and aggressive towards teachers and he once threw a chair at a teacher. As Dizzee said to *The Times,* 'I had issues as a kid. I was violent and disruptive. The way my mum helped was by finding me a different school every time I got kicked out, always fighting to keep me in the school system. Even when working two, sometimes three, jobs she never missed a parents' evening.' If it wasn't for his mother's thankless persistence, Dizzee would never have stayed in education beyond primary school, and he knows he still owes a lot to her. 'Every time I got kicked out of school my mum was heartbroken,' Dizzee told the *Sun.* 'As soon as I was expelled – and that was a lot of times – she would move heaven and earth to get me into another school. To her, education was really important, and I learned a lot from her.'

But despite his mother's continued support, Dizzee couldn't keep out of trouble, always finding himself cast as the naughty 'Boy in da Corner'. Dizzee says that his first album is all about this troublesome time.

Dizzee maintains that it wasn't always his fault, though, he felt that some teachers would pick him out because of his reputation, which wasn't helped by his manner. He told the *Observer,* 'I might have had a bit of a bad attitude. I can admit that. But a lot of it was that they kept pointing me out so, a lot of the time, any little thing I did was highlighted.'

Throughout this period, Dizzee felt that school was mostly a waste of time. He liked IT and English, both skills he uses today in making his music and writing his lyrics, and he was also into sports and athletics as a young boy. 'I did the 200 metres, 400 metres, 600 metres, 800 metres, 1,600 metres' says Dizzee. 'I ran for the Tower Hamlets borough a couple of times. I used to train after school, but from the age of thirteen I started taking music seriously and put everything else on ice.' Also, bad habits crept into his lifestyle, which inhibited his sporting dreams. 'When you're naughty, schools give up on you and stop taking you to things,' says Dizzee. 'Plus, I started smoking a bit of this and that…'

Dizzee's mother recognised that he had a talent for the arts and performing through his passion for music, so she decided to enrol him in after-school acting classes to help keep him out of trouble and channel his creative energies. The classes worked on improvisation, script work, acting exercises, dancing and singing, and the kids often had the opportunity to create short performance pieces of their own. Dizzee remembers it fondly, but he always knew music was where his passions lay: 'I went to Anna Scher for a couple of months. It's in Angel. Martin from *EastEnders*, he was in my class. But I chose music in the end. This was 2000, for about five months. I think Asher D went there… But music is my driving force, though I'm down for anything creative.'

This helped get Dizzee's creative juices flowing for when he would perform in music videos in the future, but he doesn't see himself moving into the acting industry like many US rap stars, he told *Uncensored Interview*, 'I don't really care about the whole film thing. I'm happy doing videos 'cos I get to act and play roles and that.'

Dizzee's mum knew that a few acting classes weren't going to change everything, though, and after a long line of expulsions, she eventually found him a place at Langdon Park Secondary School in Tower Hamlets.

It was an inner-city school with a lot of troubled kids, and it was given a harsh description by the *Guardian* in 2003: 'Today if you return to Langdon Park the football pitch is a dustbowl… The school bridge over the Docklands Light Railway is encased in barbed wire.' Despite most of the kids coming from some of the poorest families in Britain, the school stands in the shadows of iconic London buildings such as St Paul's Cathedral and the Gherkin, where one of the world's wealthiest financial centres turns over billions of pounds a day. Some of the big banks found in London's Square Mile donate money to the local schools, and as a result Langdon Park could afford a few computers, upon which its students could compose music. It was in one of these classes and in front of one of these computers that Dizzee would meet someone who would help him turn his life around.

Tim Smith, or Mr Smith as his pupils know him, was a music teacher at Dizzee's newest school. At the time Dizzee was a troubled young fourteen-year-old, wondering how long he'd manage to stay in this school. Mr Smith ran a relaxed class environment where he tried not to push things onto the children, his theory being that kids could come into his music class and work on the music that inspired them, whatever that was. As a result, Mr Smith's classes didn't involve much Mozart or Bach. 'I try to let students do what they want,' Mr Smith explained to the *Observer*. 'I aim to create an atmosphere where they feel safe and can experiment. My attitude is, "Show me what you can and let's work on that", rather than, "This is what we're going to do."'

Before Dizzee even got on the music department's computers, though, he used to bang away on the school's drum kit, releasing all his pent-up aggression: 'I never got taught to use the computer but I got on it from first playing the drums – I used to love playing the drums. And I DJ'd even before I touched the computer.'

Mr Smith's teaching method was aimed at encouraging the students, which had a very positive effect on Dizzee's attitude in class. 'There wasn't a problem with Dylan's behaviour in my class. OK, he had a reputation, but it didn't mean anything,' says Mr Smith. Sadly, Dizzee's reformed attitude in Mr Smith's music class didn't translate to the rest of his studies and he ended up being kicked out of his other classes. Thankfully the headmaster of Langdon Park recognised that Dizzee was making some progress, if only in music class, and didn't expel him for the trouble he'd caused elsewhere. 'The head teacher was very supportive of Dylan and me,' says Mr Smith. 'Even though there were issues in other classes.' Dizzee agrees that he responded well to Mr Smith's relaxed but encouraging teaching methods: 'In Mr Smith's class there weren't any problems. I never had an attitude in his lesson. In the past I'd made up my mind about someone as soon as I met them, so I liked or disliked them straightaway. But I got on with him from the start; he just let me get on with things.'

Most importantly, Mr Smith recognised that Dizzee had a gift, a talent for music. 'He didn't need much help. He knew what he wanted to achieve and he worked quickly. He was noticeably better than the others because his music had a clear structure and pattern, an amazing balance between rhythm, bass and melody.'

Even Dizzee's long-suffering mother was beginning to see a glimmer of hope in her troublesome child. 'Sometimes when his mum had been called in about his behaviour, I would meet her afterwards and play her Dylan's latest composition to cheer her up,' says a sympathetic Mr Smith.

Eventually Dizzee got in so much trouble in his other classes that he only attended Mr Smith's class. In fact, they got on so well he even ended up joining Mr Smith's tutor group. Mr Smith really encouraged Dizzee's passion for music, which gave him the confidence to pursue his musical dream: 'I was in danger of being thrown out of Langdon Park and, in the end, the music class was about the only one I went to because I had been excluded from most of the others,' says Dizzee. 'In the other departments they didn't really want to keep me there and eventually I joined Tim Smith's tutor group as well. Sometimes we talked about school issues but mostly it was about music. He gave me a lot of time and freedom in the classes. At playtime and lunchtime I always wanted to keep on working on my music.'

Over time Dizzee learned to respect Mr Smith, and as he unearthed his musical passion his anger at the system began to subside. 'He was my teacher; age didn't matter, I respected him,' says Dizzee. 'He understood my music and understood what I was trying to do, so nothing else mattered. If he suggested that

I listen to something I would, sometimes he gave me music or videos to watch as well.'

If it wasn't for this breakthrough, Dizzee would never have made it as a musician. It was here, in a small music class in an inner-city school, that the seeds of his musical talent were sown and Dizzee's life began to take a new direction: 'School would have been pretty dead really for me without music,' Dizzee says. 'I liked IT, and English was all right, but that was it. Everything started there; I mastered my style in that little back room.' Dizzee ended up staying at Langdon Park until the end of Year 12, over two years after being expelled from his previous school and a bit of a record for the rebellious adolescent.

Years later Mr Smith sent Dizzee his old music files from school, which Dizzee has yet to listen to: 'I've never listened to them. I might go listen to them, though.'

On a sunny August day a couple of months before Dizzee's seventeenth birthday, he got a letter through the post from the local examination board. He'd got an A in his GCSE music exam.

4

BOW SELECTA

Back in the day, Dizzee wasn't the only kid in Bow dreaming of making something of himself and getting out of the estates. Lack of a decent education meant that music or sports were what most of the kids pinned their hopes on. But all too often drugs, gangs and violence would get in the way of those aspirations. These are all issues not easily solved, Dizzee tells the *Independent*: 'I don't know the answers to all the problems there, but for individuals, I'd say, "Find something that you want to do and chase it until you get it." Music was what I chased.'

Well, he chased music and girls. He was always popular with the girls in Bow, apparently, and he used his musical knowledge to win them over. 'When I was a kid I had my slow jams tapes, of course. Have it ready, man. Ha ha. Would I ever put on one of my own tunes? Nah, that's going a bit far for me!'

Dizzee knows now that the key to getting out and making something of yourself is to work hard and stay out of trouble, but he wasn't always so wise, and it took the help of some strong figures to keep him on the right path. 'I don't think I was ever really a normal kid,' Dizzee told the *Daily Telegraph*. 'I always wanted to do it big, and so I was always on the lookout for strong people I could learn from. I suppose wanting a father figure was a part of that, but it was also that I was always searching for something more.'

But it wasn't all doom and gloom during Dizzee's childhood. He was generally quite a vivacious kid with a loud sense of humour. Even back then he had the same outlandish, extrovert sense of style he has today. In 2007 he told the *Daily Mail*, 'At fourteen I thought I looked amazing in orange jeans, fluorescent blue trainers and a green shirt. I look back and wonder what I was on. Planet Colour-blind?'

Dizzee had to make the best of whatever clothes he got given, as almost everything he wore was passed on to him by other mothers on the estate. He's learned to maintain that sense of communal generosity today and always hands his old clothes on to others: 'As a kid growing up on a council estate in Bow I always got hand-me-downs. That means that I am very careful to pass on clothes that I don't wear any more, so my cousins and my friends get all my old clothes. I was an only child so my stuff wasn't even given to me by my brothers, just by people in the neighbourhood.'

No matter how hard Dizzee's mother worked at trying to keep him on the straight and narrow, they both knew that the void of not having a father figure or role model was having an adverse affect on his behaviour. As a result, and probably subconsciously, Dizzee often used to hang out with men he could look up to, such as his school music teacher, Mr Smith. He became one of Dizzee's mentors, but there were a few more.

Despite not having any older siblings or a father, Dizzee has a few mates who are like big brothers to him and who he's still very close to today. Professional footballer Danny Shittu is one of them. 'When I was younger I was really close to Daniel Shittu,' Dizzee told *The Times*. 'He grew up in my area and was like my big brother at one point, when I was fighting and all that. I was really close to him. Because there were things I couldn't tell my mum, you know?'

Just like Dizzee's father, Danny was originally Nigerian. Born in the capital, Lagos, Danny moved to Bow when he was a child and grew up on the same estate as Dizzee. Danny was five years older than Dizzee but the two used to get on because of their shared passion for music. Dizzee used to go round to Danny's house to use his turntables and the two would mix drum and base and garage tracks. At the time Danny was one of the best DJs on the estate and Dizzee used to MC with him. 'I was like his little brother and he'd let me on the mic at parties,' Dizzee told the *Daily Mirror*. But Danny had different plans for getting out of the estates and making something of himself: he planned on training hard to become a professional footballer. He was on the books of local Premiership team Charlton Athletic and had a window of opportunity to make it as a pro. Danny was smart enough to know that you've got to work hard and keep out of trouble to achieve great things, and he tried to pass this on to his young pal Dizzee. 'When I was younger I was a bit wild and Danny Shittu used to look after me, keep me in check and that,' recalls Dizzee.

In 2001 Danny moved across town to West London to play for QPR, where he began to make a big name for himself as an uncompromising defender. He made his Premiership debut when he signed for Watford and went on to play in the World Cup, representing Nigeria.

Like Dizzee, Danny has never forgotten where he comes from and he still goes back to their old stomping ground regularly to try and give something back. Danny is big on working with kids through football, to try and help them make something of themselves and keep out of trouble: 'When I grew up here [Bow], we never really had much to do,' says Danny of his old neighbourhood. 'There wasn't things to look forward to… there weren't no role models.'

The two men are now top of their respective worlds. Having made it from tough beginnings, they're proof that it's possible to attain your dreams no matter where you come from. 'If you believe you can achieve, innit?' As Dizzee would famously tell Jeremy Paxman years later. Dizzee continues to hold Danny in high regard and the pair are still mates; Dizzee recently gave a shout out to Danny when talking to Talk Sport Radio, 'When I was a kid Danny Shittu looked after me, man. That was my idol. That was my role model when I was a kid,' Dizzee recalls. 'He was the big boy on my estate. I used to run around with him. He used to look after me. He's actually really musical, as well. At one point he was a DJ, so I used to go round and use his turntables.'

Dizzee still tries to keep in touch with many of his friends from his youth. 'My real friends are still the same; we go out, we do whatever. It's as confusing for them as it is for you. People see you on the TV and that, and they forget that you're from the streets. All the public things that you get, success and other things, there's another side that people might not know too much about. They might think you're just saying these things in your lyrics. Shit does happen, you really experience these things on the streets, and success – that can be a problem. A gift and a curse, you know what I mean?'

Dizzee knows that some of the people he grew up with are still finding their way in life, though, and it's hard for him maintain ties with people who've gone down a more troublesome route. When asked by the *Independent* if he still sees his mates from the streets, he replied, 'Not all of them. It doesn't work like that, unfortunately. Some people are trying to find their calling in life and some people aren't – that's one reason why you don't see people as much.' But for Danny and Dizzee it's been easier to maintain a link because they're both successful in their own right.

When he goes back to Bow he doesn't have Danny with him for protection these days, though he might have a security detail. He has to be careful now, as there are a few people who wouldn't mind picking a fight with him. When asked by the *Daily Mirror* if he has to watch his back in Bow nowadays, he replied, 'A little bit, but probably not as much as when I lived there. I was a lot more involved then. Now I'm a visitor. I'm a patron of the Summer University where kids get to do sports, drama, music and stuff like that... I never saw myself as a role model. I just got on with what I was doing. There's some responsibility in it, but more than anything I like that people get what I'm doing.'

In their youth Dizzee and Danny would spend hours mixing records and spitting lyrics, emulating their heroes such as MCs

Skibadee, Stevie Hyper D and DJs Shy FX and Andy C. Back then, World Dance used to hold raves in the warehouses of Three Mills Island Studios in Bow, just around the corner from Dizzee's estate, where 10,000 ravers would dance till dawn in the three warehouses. In raves like this Dizzee would split his time between the garage room and the drum and bass room. Still just a young teenager, Dizzee would go and check out his favourite DJs and MCs. At the time, jungle had morphed into drum and bass, which was Dizzee's first passion. 'I wanted to become a drum and bass DJ before all of this,' Dizzee told Jonathan Ross.

The biggest drum and bass/Jungle DJ at the time for Dizzee was undoubtedly Shy FX, who was also one of his great inspirations. Just like Dizzee, Shy FX is an urban dance music pioneer. One of the first jungle DJs and producers, he jump-started the scene with the release of 'Jungle Love' in 1992, and he created one of the genre's greatest anthems with 'Original Nuttah', featuring UK Apache, in 1994. Dizzee appreciated the big MCs Skiba and Stevie Hyper D at the time, but it was DJing that really caught his interest in the early years.

Dizzee would stay up late, listening to the top drum and bass DJs on pirate radio, and whenever he could he'd go out and watch his heroes blow the roof off raves in front of thousands of people. Dizzee was desperate to learn to mix as well as them. He couldn't always use Danny Shittu's decks, so he pleaded with his mother to lend or give him the money to buy his first turntables. Eventually she caved in: 'My mum bought me my first turntables,' says Dizzee. 'I bought them off a guy called Tony. They were wooden, some big wooden decks with round pitch control. But I was proud.'

Dizzee would scrabble together whatever money he could to buy records. He had a decent collection of old-school jungle tracks like 'The Chopper', 'Fire' and Shy FX's 'Original Nuttah', but while these were classics, jungle was old news in fast-paced East London. The big beats and ragga sounds of jungle were being replaced by a high-tempo, edgier drum and bass vibe. DJs and producers like Adam F, DJ Krust, Goldie, Roni Size and DJ Hype started taking over the scene. Despite this music being the centre of Dizzee's world, it was still seen as underground by the music business and as such didn't have much, if any, mainstream recognition.

Everyone would come round to his or Danny's place as they were some of the only guys with decks, then they'd all play drum and bass until the early hours and dance around his bedroom. Dizzee was only in his early teens at this stage, but it was here that the first signs of his musical passion were revealed – even if he wasn't very good at mixing! 'I was a joke! I was clowning,' says Dizzee. 'I had decks and that in my bedroom, so people'd come to my yard to make tapes or listen to tunes. I didn't care that much about MCing. It actually started because I'd be DJing, grabbing the mic, mucking around then getting back on the decks. People started to take the piss out you more and more, and that made me do it more. That was me up to about the age of twelve. Then I started writing lyrics.'

Sometimes when mixing in his bedroom Dizzee would shake things up by dropping in a heavy-rock track. His mates thought he was mad, but Dizzee didn't care. 'People thought I was crazy,' he admits, 'and I was an attention seeker, but I always loved that music, and I was serious about trying to make them like it.' Dizzee's confidence in his eclectic tastes was instilled from his early youth and has always been evident in his music, from his rock riffs in 'Fix Up, Look Sharp' to his contemporary *Tongue n' Cheek* days.

Dizzee's always been into different types of music and has an open mind to all forms, which has heavily influenced his style. 'My favourite rap artist is probably Jay-Z,' he told *Popmatters*. 'He's got all that as a rapper. I don't think hip-hop or music has seen anything like him ever. The rapper that got me into hip-hop was Tupac, and Bone Thugs-n-Harmony before that. I was into drum and base, hardcore, techno. I really got into crunk, Cash Money, rock. I really like Guns N' Roses, Metallica… Nirvana, and I like things like DJ Assault and the whole ghetto tech thing.'

In 1997, when Dizzee was just thirteen years old, Roni Size won the Mercury Prize, the most respected music award in the industry. Roni, a black drum and bass DJ from Bristol, was the first urban music artist to win the award, beating massive acts such as Radiohead, Spice Girls and The Prodigy. As a result, drum and bass became part of the mainstream and the rules changed for urban dance artists as the industry began to acknowledge and accept their contribution to music. At the time it didn't have any effect on Dizzee, but the sea change in attitude towards his kind of music would pave the way for his world domination in years to come.

Meanwhile Dizzee, oblivious to these changes, was heavily into listening to drum and bass and jungle. The UK was being taken over by the big commercial raves such as One Nation, AWOL and World Dance, but Dizzee preferred to go to the darker, edgier raves found in East London. 'I'm from the rave, even before Ministry of Sound, before any of that I was on the scene,' Dizzee told *Dummy* magazine. 'Caesars, Stratford Rex, The Palace Pavilion: the gutter raves.'

These raves weren't like the acid house 'free love' parties of the late eighties and early nineties, they were moody and edgy; an altogether more hardcore experience. The raves weren't always the safest place and a young Dizzee would regularly witness gun violence. Once a man was killed in front of him at a rave. 'There is a lot of shooting. I've seen people getting shot, stabbed,' says Dizzee. 'All kinds of shit. It's not a game.'

While music was one of the only positive things going for him at school, the rave scene had a massive effect on his attendance. 'I'd go to school in the morning and I was so tired,' says Dizzee. 'So I stopped giving a shit about lessons. I used to bunk off and do music.'

At home Dizzee was big into mixing drum and bass tracks, but he was also into hip-hop and still cites Snoop Dogg as a favourite. Dizzee liked the blend of hip-hop and drum and base and the way MCs were taking over the scene. MC GQ, Skibadee and Fearless were the big drum and bass figures on the mic at the time. Dizzee and his mates would spit lyrics like these guys while mixing at home, copying their catchphrases like Skiba's 'Deal with the matter, deal with the proper!'

It wasn't long before Dizzee had the confidence and skills to perform live and he would turn up to any event he could and try and grab a few bars on the mic. No doubt there were a lot of egos involved and he'd have to blag, fight and plead to get his chance. 'At that time, I'd pay to get in and hang about looking for my chance to get on the mic… There's no point waiting around being polite,' Dizzee says of trying to hustle his way on to the microphone in those early days. 'You've got to grab it and tell 'em, "I'm next."'

Sure enough, once he got his hands on the mic the crowd would go off, loving his vibe. Dizzee felt worthwhile, a rare sensation, and buzzed off the fact that people appreciated his talent. But it wasn't all about performing and appreciation for Dizzee. He's always said that he's just as happy laying down tracks in a studio as he is in front of a crowd with a mic in his hand. Even back then he enjoyed making beats and sounds in Mr Smith's music class as much as spitting heavy lyrics at a rave. So long as there was music involved Dizzee was happy.

Hip-hop was another big passion of Dizzee's from the start. The UK scene wasn't great back then, as a lot of London rappers just tried to sound American. Dizzee didn't dig how UK rappers weren't keeping it real, trying to act like they were US gangsters from the 'hood instead of getting into the UK scene. Nevertheless Dizzee used to try and catch the US stars when they came to London and caught an Eminem and D12 gig at the London Arena once.

Throughout the nineties Dizzee was listening to US rappers like Dr Dre, Snoop and Biggie, but one of his favourite artists in his early teens was Tupac. 'I was about thirteen or fourteen and having a lot of issues at school after being expelled a number of times.' Dizzee told the *Daily Mail*. 'I used to bunk off with my friends and we'd sit round listening to Tupac.' His favourite track during this period was 'All Eyez On Me'.

Another big influence on Dizzee was rock music, more specifically Nirvana. Much to the annoyance of his urban music-loving peers, Dizzee would buy rock magazines like *Kerrang!*, showing how obsessed he was with all forms of music. He still really likes 'Smells Like Teen Spirit' to this day. 'Obviously I'm not supposed to like this "because I is black", but the first time I heard it I was really moved,' he admits. 'It got me into listening to different types of music.' It's this open-minded attitude that has helped to shape Dizzee's career, and he went on to use the Nirvana track in a mash-up with 'Stand Up Tall' years later on a now infamous performance on *Later With Jools Holland*.

5

SOUND OF THE UNDERGOUND

By the late nineties Dizzee – who was going by the MC name Dizzy D – was making a name for himself amongst the DJs and MCs. But his main love, drum and bass, was on the decline as it was taken over by garage. At most of the jungle and drum and bass raves there was usually a smaller garage room, but during the nineties garage became more and more popular, especially in London. People like MJ Cole, DJ Luck and MC Neat were leaders of the scene, which prided itself on being smarter, slicker and more mature than the rough-around-the-edges drum and bass scene Dizzee was into.

By the time Dizzee got into making music seriously, in the late nineties, garage was the big new sound. However, unlike drum and bass, the mainstream gobbled up the light-hearted garage sound and it wasn't uncommon to see garage tracks in the pop charts.

The scene became centred on smart clothes and heavy attitude, which Dizzee couldn't connect with. 'I couldn't even get into the garage raves. I didn't have the clothes or the attitude,' says Dizzee. 'But I wanted to make different kinds of tunes. I'll always attempt to make a different tune.' At this time Dizzee and his mates were disillusioned with the direction garage had taken. He was still into drum and bass, but it was yesterday's news and he wanted to make music that was relevant to the streets he came from, something with a more genuine edge than the two-step and garage that dominated the airwaves at the turn of the millennium.

With garage being played everywhere from national radio to television commercials, the streets and estates of East London began developing new, unheard underground sounds. There weren't any names or labels for it at this stage, but the pioneers of this new urban sound were the inner-city pirate radio stations. Dizzee would go to estates all over the capital, especially in North London, to try and get some airtime wherever he could. 'The stations were in tower blocks, flats and industrial estates,' Dizzee told the *Sun*. 'The set-up was basic. We'd do shows from studios in the kitchen, the bedroom, the living room – basically wherever there was room to set up the equipment. I worked late, sometimes until 3 or 4a.m. I suppose pirate radio was like my *X Factor*. It gave me a chance to play my own music and learn how to freestyle and MC. It was my way of being discovered.'

The biggest of the pirate radio stations in London was Rinse FM. The legendary DJ Geeneus founded it in 1994, starting off by transmitting jungle from various East End tower blocks. Now a recognised, legitimate station, back in the day Geeneus was constantly on the run from the police, setting up his radio station with a transmitter and decks anywhere from a mate's bedroom to his grandmother's house.

A young Dizzee would tune into Rinse most nights and listen to his favourite drum and bass, garage and dubstep artists. Dizzee was beginning to realise that going to raves would only get him so far, and that if he was ever going to make any progress he would have to get himself – either through MCing or DJing – onto the airwaves.

Dizzee had to spend a long time working the circuit of lesser pirate stations than Rinse first, and he used to knock about in North London where things were less competitive than the East End. He travelled to places like Tottenham to try and get some airtime, but it was in his native Bow that recognition would finally propel his career forward. Dizzee knew that he had to get on a respected pirate station like Rinse FM to get acknowledged by fellow DJs and MCs, so he sent them a tape and was eventually given a slot.

This was his big break, for which Dizzee will always be thankful. 'Rinse FM was inspirational and influential to my journey,' he said in Rinse FM's press release after it became a licensed station. 'Listening to my peers on the radio when I was growing up helped give me a drive, focus and subsequently an outlet for my music when otherwise there would have been none.'

Around the turn of the millennium garage was still the big sound that most people wanted to hear and many of the pirate radio stations were big into it, too. The summer of 2000 was hailed as the summer of garage, with acts like DJ Luck, MC

Neat and the Heartless Crew riding high. New to the scene, Dizzee had to go with what the pirate stations wanted, even if he wasn't really into the garage vibe and his high-tempo, yelping style of rap didn't work well with it. 'I always ended up shouting and screaming,' he told the *Guardian* of his early days on air. 'When you're on pirate radio, when the speakers are blaring and everything's loud and in your face, you have to shout. I just didn't sound good over garage. I had to produce my own beats, because I didn't really fit.'

It wasn't just the sound of garage that Dizzee didn't like, the whole vibe wasn't his thing. 'Garage got to the point where it was almost bourgie – suits, shoes. A kid like me couldn't get into garage raves,' Dizzee told *CBC*. 'So a new wave of music came in.'

With garage going overground and not suiting Dizzee's flow, there was a void, both personally and as whole, on the underground scene. A void that would be filled by a new sound, one that was craved by Dizzee and the kids making urban music at the time. The sound was so fresh it didn't have a name at the time, but in the year ahead it would become known as 'grime'.

The nameless sound was being described as 'twisted', 'unmelodic', 'choppy' and 'off-centre'. Some called it 'sublow' and 'eskibeat', but whatever it was called, it represented the streets with its raw, rough beats that matched the environment at the time.

Around 2000/2001, in the more commercialised garage scene it was common for DJs and MCs to group together into crews. The big man on the music scene in Bow was Wiley, who merged Ladies Hit Squad and the Pay As U Go Cartel to make one of the biggest underground crews, although due to internal disputes they disbanded almost as quickly as they formed. The most successful crew on the scene at the time, though, were So Solid Crew, who achieved mainstream success when they hit the top of the charts with '21 Seconds To Go'.

Wiley, or Wiley Kat as he was known in his garage days, was one of the pioneers credited with starting this new underground movement. Just like Dizzee, he grew up in Bow and was a big MC in the London jungle scene of the mid-nineties. He would regularly perform with the likes of DJ Trend and Target and MC Eksman. He and DJ Target then got into the garage scene, founding The Hit Squad with MC Maxwell D. At this time they would get regular airtime on radio stations like Rinse FM, and Dizzee would listen in. Being from Bow, Dizzee knew of Wiley and looked up to him as someone older and more established in the music scene.

Speaking to the Roll Deep website in 2003 before his infamous fallout with Dizzee, Wiley recalls, 'He was like just a little boy from the area.' But even as a kid, Dizzee's wide range of musical skills made a lasting impression. 'He was like energy, raring to go. He put something back into me that I never had in me at the time. I wasn't converted to an artist, that's one thing. And I was just an MC. Listening to him made me convert to an artist, it made me open up my mind that it's not just about garage. It's music, just make music. Before that I didn't have it in me, but I got energy from him. When he was growing up listening to me it was vice versa.'

The various crews around London, including Wiley's, would meet up and do pirate radio shows together, usually at the top of council blocks, which gave them good antenna access and a great vantage point from which to look out for the police. Initially Dizzee knocked about with different crews, but eventually he found a bunch called Roll Deep, headed by Wiley. The entourage that made up the crew at the time included Biggie Pitbull, Scratchy, Breeze, Jet Li, Bubbles, Flow Dan and Jamakabi, and went on to include Tinchy Stryder in the future.

Dizzee dug the sound they were creating and was keen to get in on the Roll Deep vibe, so he pursued Wiley with a view to joining his crew. 'I'd been bothering Wiley for ages, man,' Dizzee remembers. 'He just thought, "Ah, little kid in the area." He probably didn't take me serious, but you come to the point where you stop talking and just do.'

The crew was part of a new vibe that was going on in East London at the time. Rival crews would go to raves, clubs, social clubs and pirate radio stations to project the new underground sound, which started off with a nasty edge. 'The scene turned really, really lawless,' Dizzee says. 'People definitely get shot, stabbed. London, especially right now, is a town where there's a lot of mad shit goin' on.'

With Wiley's old skool and garage connections, he got Roll Deep slots at raves all over the country, and Dizzee started to get some recognised stage time, even if it did mean he was worrying his poor mother at home. 'We was doing raves from when I was sixteen, seventeen – going up and down the country,' says Dizzee. 'Sometimes doing two or three raves in one night. I was always coming home at six o'clock in the morning. I'm sure my mum thought I was selling drugs.'

Many of the raves weren't quite ready for the dirty off-kilter beats Dizzee was making at the time. In the early days, Roll Deep was more of a garage act than anything else. One of their biggest tracks was 'Bounce', a fun garage track that got lapped up by the crowds at every rave they went to.

Aged seventeen and just about to start college, Dizzee had reached a crossroads in his life. Roll Deep was getting a name for itself as one of the best crews on the underground scene, but all the raves and late nights were taking up a lot of Dizzee's time. In the end he felt it would be too much to take on studying and a music career, so he decided to focus his attention exclusively on music. 'I dropped out of college when I was seventeen,' he told *The Student Pocket Guide*. 'And I think... that's when it seriously took over and I thought, I ain't going to college no more. I'm gonna be in the studio all of the time and I'm gonna go to all the raves.'

While dropping out of college might not have been the smartest move on the face of it, Dizzee had confidence that music would be the making of him. Some of the kids he grew up with on the estate were moving on from petty thieving into more serious crime.

'To an extent music has saved me because it was the right choice to make,' explains Dizzee. 'Around sixteen, seventeen years old I was doing both, doing the usual bullshit, but I was still going on pirate radio, I was still trying to do raves and get in the studio whenever I could. It came to a time when it was like, what is the point of all this bullshit anyway? Then I just stuck solely with the music.'

With this new single-minded attitude he started making a bit of money from performing at raves, which kept him away from trouble and saved him from pursuing crime as a career. Dizzee knew he had to focus all his attention on music and not get sidetracked by the distractions of the street.

6

OFF 2 WORK

Dizzee's would-be mentor, Wiley, had been knocking around the underground scene long enough to realise that he wasn't going to make a massive career for himself by just being an MC. The garage scene was waning and Dizzee and Wiley decided that they had to broaden their horizons musically.

So the two got stuck into making music with the rest of Roll Deep. But Dizzee needed a studio, he couldn't use the school equipment any more, and anyway, he needed something more professional. Roll Deep had made enough money from live shows to buy a bit of studio time and Wiley had connections with a local producer who had access to a studio. It was during this studio recording of the Roll Deep track 'Bounce' that Dizzee met one of his greatest mentors and friends, the producer Nick Cage.

Dizzee was younger than the rest of Roll Deep and was

very much the impressionable kid. Aged thirty-eight, Nick Cage recalled his first meeting with Dizzee to the *Observer*: 'He was baffled by things,' he remembers. 'The first time I met him he came to the studio for a session and there was a load of other people there. He just went outside and sat on a chemical waste bin that was out the back for four hours, silent, deep in thought. There were many things he was trying to work out. When you are sixteen that's always the case, but throw in poverty, the place he lived and some very strong weed and then there are no end of voices in your head.' Nick recognised that Dizzee was very smart, too smart to carry on living within the limits of the street, and that he needed help venting his obvious talents: 'The thing about Dizzee was that he was living street life, but he was extremely clever. And there is nothing worse than being clever or creative and having no outlet, or being in peer groups where people think you are weird if you want to work hard at something.'

Nick Cage produced Roll Deep's 'Bounce', a dark garage track with hints of the grime sound that was to come from Wiley and Dizzee. The track is one of the first recordings with Dizzee's voice on it. With his unique machine-gun-like flow, the track was one of the underground hits of 2002. Nick was so impressed with Roll Deep that he was keen to manage both Wiley and Dizzee, in particular Dizzee, who he felt a certain paternal protectiveness towards.

At first it would have appeared that Wiley was the most talented one with the biggest future ahead of him. After all, Wiley had been MCing for years in various scenes from jungle to garage, he had all the old-skool connections and was the main man in the East End garage scene at the time. To date, he'd made a couple of tracks with Pay As U Go Cartel and DJ Geeneus from Rinse FM, but most of this had been on a garage tip.

Looking beyond the bounds of a two-step garage beat, Wiley went to work on a new rhythm and sound, and in 2002 he came out of the studio with a track that would change the underground landscape for the next decade.

Musically, Wiley had given hints of this darker musical direction in previous years when he'd MC'd on 'Know We' with Pay As U Go Cartel. This darker form of garage, known as 'tower block two-step', was the start of taking the genre down a deeper, heavier route. The track is hailed as a classic, and is especially poignant, with Wiley foretelling that it was just the start of things to come in his lyrics, 'My time's near or I wouldn't be here, phase one, first stage of my career.'

In 2002, Wiley dropped 'Eskimo' on the world, releasing it on white label. DJ Geeneus at Rinse FM and the rest of the major players on pirate radio around London picked up on it almost immediately. 'Eskimo' was a watershed anthem, after which urban dance music would never be the same. *Stylus* magazine referred to it as 'the "Smells Like Teen Spirit" of grime.' Not that the term 'grime' had even been coined as yet. Speaking to *Jockey Slut*, Wiley described his ground-breaking genre: 'I call my sound "eskibeat". That's what I call it and everyone else can call their sound whatever they want. So people who make similar music to me, it will go under that anyway.' The now infamous 'Wiley base', a hollow whoosh sound that's synonymous with all grime today, had been intro-duced to the world – or the London underground, at least – coupled with irregular tinny clanks and chimes. The new sound was raw, unhinged and game-changing: '"Eskimo" blew the rules apart and created an environment where just about anything goes, musically.'

What followed was a major shift in urban music, all but killing off the garage scene and blowing up a new world of music born out of the streets of East London. Soon to follow would be the likes of More Fire Crew, D Double and Kano, all major players in the grime revolution of the early noughties. Not that anyone called it grime in those days, especially Dizzee, who's too much of a musical purist to label the sound. 'Everyone called it grime, but I didn't,' Dizzee told the *Guardian*. 'It was a mixture of all the stuff I was into. There is no such thing as grime. It's like hip-hop – journalists make it up. Grime is just a name that's from grimy areas and a lot of grimy shit happening, but as for the music, it's everything from reggae to drum and bass to Nirvana.'

What made early grime so appealing was that it was a direct line from the kids on the street. It was as raw and as close to the bone as music could get. 'It was just a bunch of kids whose only avenues were pirate radio and the kind of raves that no journalists would ever go to,' Dizzee says. 'And the music was just the next step on from garage and drum and bass, for all the kids who couldn't get into clubs because they didn't have the suit and the shoes. We were street boys, talking about what we knew.'

Wiley almost immediately went on to release more remixes of the revolutionary 'Eskimo' track and the other massive underground tunes such as 'Igloo' and 'Ice Rink', maintaining a fierce, harsh feel to his music. 'I'm a winter person but the cold… sometimes I just feel cold-hearted,' says Wiley. 'I felt cold at that time, towards my family, towards everyone. That's why I used those names. I was going to use "North Pole" but I didn't even get that far. It was all things that were cold because that's how I was feeling. There are times when I feel warm. I am a nice person but sometimes I switch off and I'm just cold. I feel angry and cold.'

By late 2002 Wiley was being hailed as the pioneer of grime, eskibeat or whatever it was called. By some people he was given the title the 'Godfather of Grime'. Dizzee later disputed that Wiley's track was the first grime song ever made, though, claiming that he laid down the first grime beats, inspired by southern US hip-hop, crunk: 'If you want the first grime tune it's called "Crime" and it sampled Three 6 Mafia. Grime and crunk are like cousins. Who did "Crime?" I did.'

Before these claims were made, Dizzee and Wiley were content to spur the new scene on. The two would MC together at legendary raves such Sidewinder with DJ Slimzee, the recordings of which have gone down in the annals of grime history. But cracks started to appear in the relationship between Dizzee and his peers, especially Wiley, as Dizzee 'started getting better than people', he recalled to the *Observer*. 'Let's be real, that's what happened.'

Nick Cage was always impressed with Dizzee because of his spark and natural musical ability. 'He was awake, that's what I thought, cos I was around a lot of very sleepy people. Everyone's sitting there in a coma, and he gets more work done in ten minutes than they did in two days... But then he started smoking.'

Dizzee would smoke weed quite heavily to impress his older peers in Roll Deep, but it wasn't always to the best ends.

'You've got to remember', says Cage, 'that Dizzee's in a group where people are four, five years older than him. Obviously he's got to overcompensate for being young and being the whipping boy.'

On their first meeting, during the recording of 'Bounce', Dizzee hit the weed too hard – 'I went at it – it was a challenge' – and had to go and sit outside because he started spinning out.

'The next thing I knew,' Cage says, 'he went outside and sat down in the middle of this chemical dump by the factory next door... I suppose I felt paternal towards Dizzee. Probably because no one else did. He was in bits really.'

Nick Cage would look out for Dizzee from that moment on, and Nick was also the guiding light in Wiley's fledgling career as, under the same management, the two artists started to take the underground by storm. Soon it would be the world.

As BBC 1Xtra presenter and Def Jam A&R DJ Semtex would say about the two artists, 'I think what Diz and Wiley have done is beautiful. They've put East London on the map.'

Dizzee saw the respect and success that Wiley had garnered after releasing his track, 'Eskimo' and decided that, aged seventeen, he wanted to release some of his own music on white label. He had stacks of recordings from over the years, but Dizzee worked on one of his rawest tracks which he'd made just a year earlier, 'I Luv U'. The track is about a girl getting pregnant aged fifteen, a situation he witnessed frequently on his estate. The biographical social-commentary was the first sign of what would define Dizzee's early style. Dizzee has always professed to keep it real and writes about his surroundings, experiences and pretty much what he sees in front of him.

Dizzee came up with the lyrics initially when rapping over another track, a method he uses quite frequently when making his music. 'I would rap over someone else's songs to practice and get a lot of my lyrics out,' he told *'Sup Magazine*. 'For "I Luv U," I wrote that to "Is That Your Chick" [2000 single from Memphis Bleek featuring Jay-Z, Missy Elliott and Twista].'

When it came to laying down the track, it took Dizzee only twenty minutes. Normally artists take days, weeks, even months to get a tune right. Dizzee's time spent in the classroom learning his skills were paying off, putting him way ahead of the game at a young age. 'It's all a continuation from school, just using computers… databases and that, straight to learning Cubase,' explains Dizzee. 'It's just the more you do anything the better you become. I learnt to make beats quick, do it, get it out the way – other people spend three days on one tune, wasting their time!'

So Dizzee laid down his first track in a matter of minutes, produced it himself on white label and wasted no time in hustling it, just like his mother used to, when she'd go around the estate selling clothes. Dizzee went to all the local East London DJs to get the track played on pirate radio, at raves, wherever – just so long he got his sound out there. 'Just got the dubs and took them round to the DJs,' says Dizzee. 'Five hundred white labels first and it sold all together on the under-ground about six thousand.'

The track has a rough, dark baseline and the skewed beat that's now so associated with grime. Peppered with Dizzee's adolescent rapping, the song felt immersed in the sort of angst and fear that only a teenager from the estates can feel and create.

'I Love U' was later hailed by some as one of the first ever grime tracks, despite Wiley's 'Eskimo' previously getting the plaudits. Dizzee went on to claim that 'I Love U' came first: '"I Luv U" came before "Eskimo." Wiley was making garage, really good vocal garage.' The dispute was just one of many that would destroy their friendship.

Everything was going great for Dizzee when his debut track came out, and soon enough the pirate airwaves of London were buzzing with the sound of 'I Luv U'. It wasn't long before the internet caught hold of it, too. Unlike today, the internet was an unknown quantity for the music industry. For the most part it was distrusted by label bigwigs, who just saw it as a means for people to steal music without them making any money. But for Dizzee and his early fans it was another way for him to showcase his talents – not that he knew anything about it at the time.

Music critic Simon Reynolds heard 'I Luv U' on pirate radio and was completely blown away by the groundbreaking new sound. He immediately typed the name Dizzee Rascal into Google – as we all do these days when we want to check out a new artist we've just heard – but Reynolds found nothing online. It was pre-Myspace days and, anyway, Dizzee didn't have ready access to the internet for self-promotion.

Motivated by this lack of information on the underground artists that were fast emerging, Reynolds decided to set up Blissblog to cover his kind of music. It soon got a worldwide following, and at the end of 2002 Reynolds nominated Dizzee's white label number 'I Luv U' to be his track of the year. 'The blogs had a big role in building a buzz on Dizzee outside the underground scene itself,' Reynolds told the *Guardian* in 2003. 'Someone as talented as Dizzee would rise regardless, but I do think "we" helped get things started in terms of the music media. I reckon a lot of music journalists check out the blogs.'

MP3 file-sharing was really taking off at this time and soon enough 'I Luv U' was getting out into the blogosphere and around the world. Unknown to Dizzee, his music was getting into the headphones and speakers of a lot more than just the vinyl junkies of East London.

7

DIRTEE STANK

These days, talk of labels with Dizzee usually centres around Gucci, Armani and Hugo Boss, but back then he didn't have anything flashier than Nike, so when he talked about labels he meant record labels and the music business.

For years Dizzee's older peers, such as Wiley and the rest of Roll Deep, were performing at raves and on pirate radio. They had a little cash and a name for themselves, which got respect in and around East London, and, of course, local girls knew who they were. Compared to most people on the estates they were doing pretty well. Dizzee had bigger plans. He wanted to take over the world, and to do this he'd need to get signed to a label. No label would sign an unproven artist like Dizzee, a kid from the ghetto with an attitude and a few grainy tapes as proof of his talent. Dizzee wasn't bothered, though. He decided to set up his own label, and along with his manager and producer, Nick Cage, he set up Dirtee Stank Recordings, through which he produced his first track, 'I Luv U'. The label's logo is a picture of flies circling faeces, and when asked why he chose this image he said it was the 'streetest thing I could think of'.

By the summer of 2002, the underground was charged and revitalised by the sounds of Wiley and Dizzee Rascal's new tracks, and Nick Cage was the man leading the way. Cage was constantly running around town getting them more bookings on pirate radio stations and at raves than ever before. Dizzee and Nick were also spending more and more time in the studio with the aim of getting as much music out on their independent label as possible. 'I was putting out tracks like "I Luv U" and a couple of instrumentals,' Dizzee recalled to *CBC*, 'which were around on pirate radio and the underground scene.'

There weren't any other musicians, let alone labels, making the new sound, which was why Dizzee founded the label. He wanted to create a vehicle upon which the dirty grimey tracks he was creating could be transported to the wider world. Dizzee explained his label to James Hyman on XFM shortly after founding it: 'The theory behind it is that it's the dirtiest grimiest thing you can find… it's just a label there for the streets, ya get me?' Dirtee Stank went through a few fallow years while Dizzee established his mainstream career and signed with a major label. But it's been reignited of late, with Dizzee and Nick Cage using it to help artists from the same difficult backgrounds as Dizzee.

The name for Dizzee's new label was taken from a lyric in one of his first recorded tracks, 'Bounce', which he made with Roll Deep: 'The name came from one of the first lyrics I had:

"Going on dirty/going on stank."' So I thought, "Yeah, fuck it, Dirtee Stank."'

Dizzee's new label did exactly what it was supposed to do, starting a surge of dirty, grimey beats around the streets. But it wasn't long before the more influential people in the music business began to take note of Dizzee's massive underground success. They wanted to find out about this kid who was changing the urban-music landscape, and they were desperate to get in touch with Dizzee and Nick. Finally it wasn't Dizzee who was doing the hassling, now Dizzee was being hassled.

During this period, Wiley was still rolling with Dizzee, while marketing his sound as far and wide as possible, preaching the 'Eskimo' gospel to anyone who'd listen. Wiley set up his own rave, Eskimo Dance, where himself and like-minded DJs and MCs established the origins of the grime scene. It attracted a lot of attention for the fights that went on and for being part of the 'gutter rave' movement, where crime and violence were commonplace.

Dizzee was often involved in the trouble that occurred at these raves, as lots of people had an issue with him because of his relative success at such a young age. 'Guys would come and attack him with concrete posts and bricks. And he would always face it out, take them all on,' says Nick Cage of these troublesome times.

Some of the other MCs and DJs also began to get jealous of Dizzee's many skills, DJing, MCing and producing heavy tracks. Crazy Titch was also from East London and is known as one of the best MCs from grime's very early days. He was a member of Boys In Da Hood and featured on most of the biggest pirate radio stations at about the same time as Dizzee.

Crazy Titch was similar to Dizzee as a child, a gifted young black kid from the East End estates with a sharp mind and a bad attitude. He told Chantelle Fiddy (*Mix Mag, RWD*): 'Because I was like a black sheep in my early school days, I actually read books. It was cause of that, as a young kid, I wanted to be Burglar Bill. He'd always get shifted then there'd be another book so I thought he got away with it. Really, they should ban that book and just teach them (kids) the ABC and times table.'

Titch's career started to take off around the same time as Dizzee's. He joined forces with his stepbrother Doogz (also known as Durrty Goodz) to form Boys In Da Hood. By January 2003 he had recorded his first track 'True MCs' with Doogz and N.A.S.T.Y. Crew's Hyper. Although it never got released it wasn't long before leading producer Terror Danjah (Aftershock Records) invited Titch to appear on 'Cock Back' alongside Riko, Hyper and Dizzee's long-standing friend D Double E.

His first solo release was in 2004, 'I Can C U', which was playlisted at Radio 1Xtra and is recognised as one of Channel U's most-voted-for videos and garage tracks of all time. Since then Titch has featured on Shystie's 'Make It Easy' remix (Polydor) and Mr Wong's 'Orchestral Boroughs'.

Dizzee and Crazy Titch were fierce rivals back then and used to battle it out on radio. On one infamous occasion in the late summer/early autumn of 2003, the two clashed on pirate station Deja Vu after Crazy Titch refused to hand back the mic after his allotted sixteen bars. A slanging match ensued with Dizzee repeatedly shouting at Titch, 'I'm not a mook (fool)'. A member of Roll Deep filmed the incident and released it on

DVD, calling it *Conflict*. The two had to be pulled apart and have been involved in a nasty rivalry ever since. Crazy Titch explained the incident in *Lord of the Decks*, the first professionally presented mixtape and DVD package to come out of East London's grime scene. In a bleak council flat stairwell Titch explained, 'I had loads of stuff to get off my head, I'd just come back from [Ayia] Napa. I'd lost about three stone. I was not a happy boy at all.' Titch went on to explain the trouble to Sarah Bentley of XLR8: 'Everyone was writing sly bars about each other,' explained Titch. 'I don't care about sly bars. I just say your name. Let's get the clash on. It kicked off with Dizzee 'cos he touched my arm. I was fresh from the bing (Young Offenders' Centre). There's not much personal things in the bing, so you have to respect your personal space. He invaded mine. I flipped on him. But I don't care about all that now. It's just air.'

After Dizzee's release of *Boy in da Corner*, Crazy Titch came out with the track 'Just An Arsehole' – a cover of the track 'Jus' A Rascal'. Titch explains: 'Dizzee dissed me on Westwood. I can't have that so I wrote the bars and laid it down. I didn't know how I was gonna get my tune played so I was like, "Well, I know where Radio One is, I'll just go there." Westwood didn't play it the week I left it, but then the following weekend he started rinsing it. I went down the studio a few weeks after that.'

The original Taz-produced bassline of Dizzee Rascal's anthem 'Jus' A Rascal' hollered out over Britain's airwaves in 2004 with the raucous new vocals of MC Crazy Titch. Tim Westwood, the legendary BBC Radio One hip-hop DJ, gave Crazy Titch's Dizzee Rascal-dissing dubplate three plays on the trot, exclaiming, 'Dizzee, man, maybe you should 'low it with this guy. He sounds scary.'

Getting on Radio One was a big deal for Titch – even if it was off the back of Dizzee's track – especially as he was consistently refused by pirate stations such as Rinse. 'I used to ring Rinse FM and be like, "Yeah man, I wanna spit some lyrics," and they'd be like, "You're good but, er, too violent for radio,"' remembers Titch. 'It was a joke, a style. None of it was serious. I was young and gone. I knew what would make people laugh. I talk about real-life situations now. I'm off the violence. Just don't push me.'

Dizzee responded with a 'Lean Back' cover. But it wasn't long before the pair's musical feud was brought to a premature end when Crazy Titch was sent to prison to serve a minimum of thirty years after another MC feud went too far. Titch was found guilty of being involved in a murder where a Mac-10 machinegun was used to kill an associate of a rapper who'd 'disrespected' his friend.

It was as clear a message as any that Dizzee needed to avoid these petty disagreements and concentrate on his music, and nobody knew this better than his manager, Nick Cage.

Nick Cage had been Wiley's manager for longer than he'd been Dizzee's, and he'd been trying to get him signed for a while. Now with the grime movement gaining headway, labels started showing an interest in the both of them. For Nick Cage it looked like there would be a double score if he got the two artists signed at the same time.

The big labels that came in for Dizzee included Def Jam and XL and soon enough they were trying to outbid each other in the hope of signing arguably the freshest young talent of his generation. Dizzee, cool as ever, revelled in the situation, but knew that XL was the right label for him, given their history of signing left-field acts. He felt he could rely on XL to let him be what he wanted to be without too much interference.

XL has a long history of signing left-field acts. Originally a major part of the underground acid-house scene (the equivalent of grime in the late eighties) the label specialised in the hardcore rave sounds that were coming out of London and the surrounding area. XL founder Richard Russell was a teenager, DJing on pirate radio and in clubs, as well as producing and remixing records for the underground scene, just like Dizzee. XL helped shaped an era-defining genre, the rave scene. The XL website claims that the early acid-house scene at that time was all about 'home recording, white label record releases, pirate radio and illegal raves.' Sound familiar?

One of XL's early signings was the Prodigy, pioneers of the rave scene. The creative talent of the Prodigy came in the form of a young Essex teenager, Liam Howlett, who recorded at home using borrowed samples from sources as diverse as Max Romeo, Ultramagnetic MCs and children's TV programmes. The band went on to become one of the biggest sellers of the nineties, reaching number one in twenty-six countries and establishing XL as a serious label. For the label bosses, the Prodigy's success was a massive lesson. One of XL's head producers, Richard Russell, claimed in an interview with *The Times* that letting the Prodigy develop their own music without interference was key to their success: 'We were so fortunate with our first experience being Prodigy. It's like the less palatable it was the better it was. The less palatable they got the better they did. That was my education.' It was a lesson that Dizzee would benefit from years later, as this lack of interference was exactly what he craved.

Dizzee knew that signing for XL was a natural progression for him as they got what he was about more than the other competing labels. 'It seemed like the next step,' Dizzee told XFM, just after he signed. 'The other people who I would've signed was Def Jam, innit? But, it's like XL saw the vision. And I looked at their track record and saw they done Prodigy, people like Basement Jaxx, Streets. And that's all, like, not obscure, but it's different music. So we needed someone who can understand the vision and accept us for what we was and what we do, ya get me?'

Nick and Wiley felt the same way as Dizzee and both artists signed for XL at around about the same time in 2002, with Nick saying, 'We gave Dizzee's tracks to some pirate DJs to play for quite a long time, people couldn't get their heads round it for a while, but when it clicked then we released it. Most of the labels came up and said their piece after that, we had some offers, but Richard from XL really got the music and came forward with an interesting proposition. Getting creative control over three albums is great; majors are trying to sign artists up for five or seven albums. We're building a good relationship with XL – they took the Prodigy to seven million albums from playing raves. We've come up a similar way, albeit with a different kind of music.'

Around about this time, in mid-2002, Wiley and Dizzee got a slot opening for Jay-Z at Wembley Arena. Wiley left the PA tracks behind at home and had to travel all the way from Wembley in North West London to Bow in the East End to get them. By the time Wiley got back to Wembley they'd missed their slot, but after Dizzee persuaded the promoter, he eventually let them go on stage. Dizzee told XFM how he blagged it:

'It was amazing. It was one of them mad days. We thought it weren't gonna happen. We left the CDs and the dat. Wiley left it somewhere. So we had to go out. And then Wembley was all chock-a-block. Everywhere around North West London was all just rammed. And we thought we weren't gonna get there. We came back and then we missed our spot… I had to try and find the man who was doing the show and had to hassle him.'

For Dizzee, performing wasn't the highlight. The main moment was watching the great Jay-Z: 'I was just content with standing back looking at him… He was doing what I just did but better. And for more money, obviously. That was the best part: watching him.'

The Jay-Z gig was all before Dizzee had been signed and was arranged by his long-time admirer and friend DJ Semtex, who also wanted Dizzee to sign for Def Jam, where he'd established their urban department in 2001. Dizzee described Semtex as 'just the best DJ in the country,' to *LeftLion* magazine years later. 'It's a blessing for me. He was an A&R and he was going to sign me to Def Jam and had me supporting Jay-Z when I was seventeen. When I didn't end up signing with Def Jam, he was still around, know what I mean? He's just a part of what I do. It's how we'll continue to be as well.'

In the summer of 2002 XL felt they were on to a winner with Dizzee, partly because of his underground following but also because of his online fanbase, which was growing by the day. Simon Wheeler, one of the head honchos at XL, told the *Guardian* just a year after signing Dizzee that the online buzz surrounding him in blogs and file-sharing networks was a major reassurance for the label when taking a risk on such a new artist. 'It backed up our opinion that Dizzee was someone who would inspire a lot of people once they were exposed to him… If there are people who are influential in a particular scene, you're going to want them to act as taste makers.'

XL decided to release Dizzee's underground hit, 'I Luv U' as soon as possible in the spring/summer of 2003. They gave it a bit of digital remastering and it was reproduced by Jacob Freitt and given a large-scale release. By June of that year, the debut single became Dizzee's first top 40 hit, peaking at number 29, which was OK but some people were hoping for bigger things. It's not a pop track, so it was never going to make it into the top ten. The track was still very raw and, some felt, not to the commercial end of the musical spectrum's taste. The world wasn't quite ready for Bow's sound, it would seem.

Despite the limited success of Dizzee's first single, XL charged ahead with producing his first album. They were eager to capitalise on the modest momentum he was gaining and they were convinced his material was strong enough to gain immediate success. Dizzee was seen as the label's new golden boy, and they were 100 per cent focused on making a big success of their new star.

Wiley had known Nick a lot longer than Dizzee and it must have been hard for him to sit back and watch. Wiley now accepts that Dizzee just had grander plans at the time.

In an interview in 2007 Wiley told Dan Hancox about his upset during this period. 'Dizzee's vision was further than mine at the time, and our manager had to take Dizzee to where he was going, but he left us all behind. I was in Dizzee's shadow. I was naturally jealous of him, and the label, XL, were focusing on him, and not really concerned about me. Me and Dizzee on the same label wasn't going to work: there was a conflict of interest there.' Wiley stuck with it and worked on his album, which was due for release the following year, but cracks in the pair's relationship were beginning to appear.

8

BOY IN DA CORNER

There was no stopping Dizzee now. The young star was charging ahead with his career with barely a glance to his past. His sole focus in life during the summer of 2003 – when he was still only seventeen years old – was his album. Dizzee was able to produce an album in no time at all after getting signed, mainly because he had a back catalogue of tracks that were ready to go and which demanded to be released to the wider world, so he compiled the best of them with a few more recent tracks. His sound back then was rough and raw, with Dizzee using anything and everything as influence: rock, jungle, hip-hop, whatever. He also wanted to experiment with the kind of sounds he would use. 'I'd try to build a tune in fifteen minutes using the most obscure sounds I could find – put a microphone next to a frying pan and knock it – just to see how they'd fit together,' he told the *Independent* shortly after the album's release.

Dizzee's first album, *Boy in da Corner,* hit the record shops on 16 July 2003. It was a big moment for Dizzee, and one in which he didn't forget the people who'd helped him get there. Dizzee paid tribute to his music teacher Tim Smith, who'd helped him so much at school, writing on the inside of the album sleeve remembering how it was Mr Smith who believed in him from the start. Dizzee would later tell the *Observer* that he could never forget the contribution Tim Smith made to his early music career and how he had to credit him in the album. 'Obviously Tim Smith has played a big part in my success, and the album was written to reflect how I felt and much of it came from my school days. I had to credit Mr Smith on the CD. I was never going to forget him. I'm not like that.'

Obviously Mr Smith was delighted with the credit, saying, 'I was thrilled to find out that he had credited me on his album. A journalist phoned me before I heard the album. He told me what Dizzee had written. I said, "Come on, get real." He said, "No, it's on the album." "Well, that's fantastic," I said. I was really chuffed. It's my job to help all the students, but Dylan has done particularly well. I'm very proud of him, and it's nice to be remembered.'

Dizzee's partner in grime back then, Wiley, features on the track '2 Far', and he also give him a mention on the album sleeve telling Wiley that they, 'roll deep.'

The album brought the grime scene into the public domain. The underground sound was no longer the property of white-label-hunting vinyl junkies and East End tower-block kids – those who heard *Boy in da Corner* were blown away and it made big waves in the industry almost immediately.

'I remember when Dizzee's first album leaked,' said Gavin Mueller of *Stylus* magazine. 'I huddled in front of my computer, waiting patiently for the album to finish downloading. I listened to it once, then immediately burned four copies. It was the kind of music that reminded me of why I had a craven dependence on high-speed internet and used-record stores, the kind of music that shortened my breath, caused my stomach to jump into my throat and required me to share it with everyone I could.'

People saw it as a window into the hidden world of inner-city life at the rawest level – Dizzee had achieved his aim of getting his world across to other people. 'There's so many things, really,' Dizzee says when trying to explain his album. 'It's to show people, maybe who even live where I do, what's going on around their corner – adults just think they know, but they look at it from a newspaper point of view. I'm deep in, but I've got a brain, and I don't just want people from the estate or even the country I'm from to understand.'

The mix of new sounds was like nothing most people outside of East London had ever heard and they went crazy for it. The *Independent* said it sounded like someone 'walking through London's busiest, most multicultural streets, absorbing every noise, from the bhangra or dancehall reggae coming from a car to the constant trebly chirp of mobile ringtones and car alarms, and making it into a polymorphous music, as irritating yet as stimulating as the sounds of the inner city.'

The title is a personal subject for Dizzee, as he'd always felt like the naughty child sent to sit in the corner and blocked in by the world around him. He told XFM that *Boy in da Corner* 'represents that person, anyone who feels they've ever been in a corner or boxed in: a street corner, get sent in the corner at school… anyone who feels that way and everyone feels that way sometimes.'

The album is fifty-seven minutes of edgy teenage angst, fear and depression. It's as if Dizzee bottled the first seventeen years of his life and poured it into a vinyl mould. For Dizzee, the album was cathartic – a form of therapy to help him get out his emotions. 'If you're feeling bad, it cleanses you, because the rage is in the music,' Dizzee explained to the *Independent*. 'So once the album's done, the anger's gone with it. It's been angry for you. I'd like people to think of my record from that point of view. A lot of people feel like me in this city. So they can turn it on for sixty minutes, and then get on with things.'

The album opens with 'Sittin' Here'. The track has a sinister chime and tinny beat where Dizzee's high-pitched lyrics play a central role as he talks about the trials of youth boredom and inactivity in the inner-city estates. In an interview with XFM Dizzee picks the record out as one of his favourites because 'it shows the struggle that we go through. We used to just sit around outside the off-licence, drink, smoke, chat shit, whatever. It's just harsh reality, that's what it is.'

Track two, 'Stop Dat', picks up the pace from the first track with a heavy jungle-esque baseline. This ill-tempered track betrays Dizzee's take on the more egotistical side of the music scene.

Wiley raps on the third track on the album, '2 Far'. Dizzee uses rhythmical head-nodding beats while he vents anger at marriage, police and monarchy.

Dizzee makes use of some genre-crossing rock samples in

the album in 'Fix Up, Look Sharp', where Dizzee samples US rock star Billy Squier's 'The Big Beat', demonstrating his encyclopedic knowledge of music. Dizzee's simplicity is shown in this track, where he does little more than rap over the drum rhythm of the sample. I wonder what the eighties idol and fifty-three-year-old rocker would have made of Dizzee's interpretation, which went on to be released as Dizzee's second single from the album?

In the slow, off-kilter track 'Cut 'Em Off' Dizzee has a go at kids with attitude in East London, and all the fronting, ego and silly nuances that goes with it.

Iconic garage MC God's Gift – an old friend of Wiley, from his Pay As U Go Cartel days – makes an appearance in 'Hold Your Mouf'. The track has a big baseline, where Dizzee's high-pitched rap contrasts well with God's Gift's gruff booming voice and contains the legendary lyric that seemed to sum, 'I'm a problem for Anthony Blair'.

Dizzee's sinister, loveless world is exposed in 'Round We Go', where Dizzee talks about the continual cycle of emotionless sex between everyone in his world.

The up-tempo nature of 'Jus' A Rascal' makes a welcome change to the sombre beats of the tracks that lead up to it. With a rock guitar riff, it feels like Dizzee introducing himself to the world, revealing the girtty life he's from and the more luxurious lifestyle he is looking for.

In 'Wot U On' Dizzee continues his theme of venting against the fake people and the fake almost meaningless objects that go with them inhabiting the world around him. The track uses organ-like synths in the background, making for an even eerier sound than normal.

'Jezebel' takes Dizzee to a darker place lyrically, as he raps about teenage mothers, contracting STDs and the bitterness and confusion that goes with that as well as promiscuity more generally.

Almost perversely he sets the lyrics against high-pitched pizzicato strings that chime, almost happily, throughout the track, displaying Dizzee's twisted sense of humour and musical genius.

In 'Seems 2 Be' – an almost, cheery track with funny, whimsical lyrics – Dizzee introduces a more cheeky baseline that we'll see a lot of later in his career. By the time he gets on to 'Live O' Dizzee has given up on all ideas of rhythm with what sounds like a complete mishmash of beats, reminiscent of Aphex Twin.

Dizzee signs off with 'Do It!' where he employs a slow rhythm synth and some of his most revealing lyrics, showing a teenage depression that verges on the suicidal.

Keeping the most emotional track to last ends the album on a poignant note and leaves the listener feeling as if they've had a real insight into Dizzee's hopes and fears.

Upon the album's release, XL posted a copy of their new star's record to respected music journalists all over the country. The immediate response was of shocked approval. In the September after the album's release, Gavin Mueller of *Stylus* said it 'sounds like 2010… there is NO SOUL HERE. And that's the point. Dizzee dances adeptly over the harsh sequences, easily matching every beat with vibrant flows, immersive slang and his unique voice. It's no easy task to stay above the over-driven beats, which threaten to drag Dizzee down into the gears should he let down his guard. He must keep moving or he will be trapped, a neat metaphor for the record which could be Dizzee's ticket out of the streets.'

Just two days after the album was released, Alexis Petridis of the *Guardian* wrote that Dizzee was 'the most original and exciting artist to emerge from dance music in a decade'. He described the album's sound as 'disjointed electronic pulses pass for rhythms. Above them lurch churning bass frequencies, disturbing choruses of muttering voices, clattering synthesisers that recall police sirens and arcade games… the overall effect is shocking and unsettling in the extreme.'

Petridis didn't hold out much hope of the album being a major success, though, stating that 'whether anybody will listen seems questionable. Both Dizzee Rascal's music and message are wildly unpalatable, and the British record-buying public is not currently renowned for wild risk-taking.'

Dizzee was even getting recognition in the States, normally a graveyard for British urban artists, after *Boy in da Corner* was released in the US on Matador Records in January 2004. Even if they didn't quite 'get it' and thought of it as British hip-hop, there were still very positive sounds from the US critics.

Scott Plagenhoef of *Pitchfork*, the Chicago-based internet publication renowned for seeking breakthrough acts, claimed that 'Rascal's record is an icy orchestra of scavenger sounds, owing as much to video games and ringtones as it does to anything more overtly musical. The despairing beats make the lyrical push and pull that much more severe: When Dizzee is venomous, they sharpen his bite; when he gamely searches for the light at the end of the tunnel, admits his failures, laments his unravelling psyche, and battles with depression, they seem like obstacles.' Plagenhoef goes on to compare Dizzee to some of Britain's most infamous left-field exports, claiming that his future is full of world-reaching potential: 'Dizzee's despairing wail, focused anger, and cutting sonics place him on the front lines in the battle against a stultifying Britain, just as Johnny Rotten, Pete Townsend and Morrissey have been in the past. The difference between the four (and their claims that "There's no future," "I hope I die before I get old," "I don't want to wake up on my own any more," and "I wish I could sleep for ever") isn't as different as it might appear on the surface. If Rascal grows at a similar rate, it's not out of the question that he could leave a comparable legacy.'

Also in the UK, *Interview* magazine said, 'On his debut, this UK garage-gangsta stutters over bass-heavy beats, tackling all the right subjects – urban plight, social protest, street violence – in his distinctive stop-and-go flow. While the record ventures into fresh territory, it's most accessible when it gets familiar: "Fix Up, Look Sharp," which samples the classic break from Billy Squier's "Big Beat", is a highlight.'

People magazine also commented on the album's originality, 'You have to give Rascal props for what is surely one of the most original discs to hit this side of the pond in some time.' And even *All Music Guide* heaped on praise, saying, 'Startling, tirelessly powerful, and full of unlimited dimensions, nothing could truly weigh down this debut.'

If people in the closed-minded US were taking notice of the kid from Bow, things were bound to happen. Dizzee's debut album was an instant all-time classic. As the *Independent* would later claim, '*Boy in da Corner* remains one of the great London albums, an eerie, pungent mash-up of cultures under stress, a snapshot of a young underclass being put through an economic and environmental ringer. With jokes.' However, nobody knew, not even the most respected music journalists, that this was just the tip of the iceberg for Dizzee, or how far *Boy in da Corner* would propel him.

9

GRIME WAVE

Boy in da Corner was taking the industry by storm, more for its new and refreshing sound than anything else. Those involved in pirate radio and the 'gutter raves', as Dizzee calls them, would be familiar with the edgy beat Dizzee had produced, but the mainstream hadn't heard anything like it to date and it was a big wake-up call as to what was going on in the streets. The media immediately labelled Dizzee's style of music 'grime', but this wasn't what Dizzee or his mates referred to it as. 'I'm an artist, that whole grime thing is a journalist thing,' Dizzee told *The Student Pocket Guide*. 'The music I was making back in the day was really grimy or really edgy, but I never personally had no name for it.'

Some still referred to Dizzee's music as 'garage', others as 'tribal skank', and one of the most imaginative names for it came from the States, where it was called 'euro terror techno'.

Wiley still lived in hope that his name, 'eskibeat', would catch on, but soon enough most music journalists began sticking with 'grime' as an all-encompassing name for the genre.

Commercially, *Boy in da Corner* sold reasonably well in its first few weeks. It entered the UK charts at number 40, peaking at 23, and across the pond in the US it sold 58,000 copies; that meant 250,000 worldwide and over 100,000 in the UK, earning it a gold disc. In the summer of 2003 Dizzee was on course for superstardom – until a trip to Ayia Napa almost ended everything.

In the late nineties Ayia Napa, on the eastern edge of Cyprus, became the summer party venue for everyone involved in the garage scene. And when DJ Nick Power of Kiss FM opened Kool Club there in 1995, the resort became an urban alternative to the house-music-orientated Ibiza. Since then, all the big garage and urban music DJs went out there every summer to play blockbuster sets at the best summer parties.

By the summer of 2003 the place was heaving with garage enthusiasts and their crews. Head of the Ayia Napa music scene at this time was So Solid Crew, and their leader, Megaman, was the godfather of the island – they couldn't walk through the town without being mobbed for pictures and autographs. So Solid's highlight was the legendary weekly show, where every Sunday night they played to a sellout 1,300-capacity crowd at Club Ice. For many UK fans it was their only chance to see So Solid Crew.

Notorious local movers the Cypriot Melas brothers owned the biggest club in town, Club Ice, and garage acts were a regular fixture on the bill. Unfortunately, that summer plenty of violence spread through Ayia Napa, with stabbings between rival gangs becoming a regular occurrence.

In the summer of 2003, police increased their nightly patrols around the town in order to combat the violence problems. A local at the time told journalist Nick Webster that there was a lot of concern in the town: 'It's exactly the same as football hooliganism. It's not the team causing the trouble but the fans. Except it is worse because garage is about attitude. It's a lifestyle, not just music, for them.'

It was looking like violence would play a part in the summer of 2003 in Ayia Napa, and a young Dizzee had just arrived. In the first week of July 2003 – the same week that *Boy in da Corner* had been released – Dizzee and the Roll Deep Crew went out to Ayia Napa to perform. Dizzee's debut solo album had recently been released, he'd just returned from LA where he was filming the video for 'Fix Up' and life was good. Dizzee spent his time at the Cypriot beach resort chatting up girls on the beach, partying by night and checking out some of the other musical acts that were playing in town – one of the biggest of which was the infamous So Solid Crew.

Originally from South London, the garage collective So Solid Crew had grown up on the pirate radio circuit, just like Dizzee. Underground stations such as Supreme and Delight FM were big supporters of the South London garage scene then, and the crew made their biggest impact on Delight with their regular Sunday slot, 'So Solid Sundays'. The radio show's massive popularity saw the group achieve huge success in 2001, when they signed a record deal and released the number one hit '21 Seconds'. For the first few years of the noughties, So Solid were the biggest act in the garage and urban music scene. So when a talented new guy arrived – in the form of Dizzee Rascal – some people weren't too happy.

Asher D was one of the main rappers in So Solid Crew. In 2002, he was sentenced to eighteen months in prison after being caught with a loaded gun. He was released early for good behaviour. But by the time he was released there must have been a great deal of talk about how Dizzee had become the biggest street superstar.

Asher had a lot of reservations about the scene when he came out of prison, and he started dissing a lot of the big names at the time. In an interview with *RWD* magazine, Asher said, 'I listened to Dreem Teem a couple of times but they did nothing for me, they don't do nothing for no one in jail – I know that for a fact. They're whack. For me, it was all about Westwood, I'm feeling 50 Cent.'

Asher felt that all of the new crews at the time were just imitating his So Solid Crew. 'Anyone who comes out now will be seen as a follower, you get me? They'll get compared to us and they'll start to hate us. But So Solid is a household name now. I'm cool with the garage and the new crews and that, but know your place, man, stop it. I don't wanna sound big headed, even though I am, but there is a line there, we're [So Solid Crew] separate now, different.'

Asher started directing his criticism at the new kid on the block, Dizzee, saying that his music was 'weak' and how he was above and beyond Dizzee as an artist. 'I get this rubbish every day, man, like, "Oh, have you heard that Dizzee Rascal boy coming up? He's competition you know, Asher?" Dizzee's seventeen years old... the production, man, it's like I wanna throw up, it's old. That's "21 Seconds" production. We've been there already, it's old now. He's not on my level, people should stop comparing me to him. I will drop a chorus that'll end his whole career!'

Dizzee heard all this and there was a subsequent MC battle arranged on Choice FM, where the two fought one of the most legendary MC duels of all time. Dizzee put down Asher with his lyrics saying he was on another level.

It wasn't long before the online forums were filling up with praise for the young MC after the battle. But Asher had some support too and he still thinks he got the better of Dizzee, telling *Blues and Soul* online magazine, 'I won it and that's that.' Many others, including Dizzee, disagreed. Dizzee didn't feel the beef with Asher D was anything major and told XFM, 'It's nothing, it's entertainment… anytime anyone wants anything, I'm around.'

Speaking about it in September 2003 to the *Guardian*, Dizzee was adamant that he never wanted any trouble or that he ever started anything. 'Asher D dissed me first. I would never call somebody out for no reason. It's not in my nature. He came out of prison and he started talking. In that whole garage scene, I've always been one to do my own thing. They can have their little wars and that, MCs clashing, whatever.'

There are various versions of what occurred later that year in Cyprus, but the end result was that Dizzee was reportedly stabbed five or six times in the chest, back and bum. He still has the brutal scars today, but is reluctant to go into the full story. One DJ, who was there but refused to be named, told journalist Nick Webster that it was So Solid Crew fans who'd stabbed Dizzee: 'It all kicked off when Dizzee pinched Lisa Maffia's arse. But he's only a kid and they're older, so they shouldn't have done it. They beat him up and the two crews started fighting. No knives or anything, though. Then later in the day they had a meeting to sort things. But some of the fans didn't hear about the meeting, so Dizzee was stabbed. The followers of the two crews hate each other.'

Others thought that the older generation of MCs and DJs were jealous of the new young star. Michael Brown of urban music magazine *Tense* says, 'Dizzee Rascal is the new kid on the block. There must have been a bit of the green eye of jealousy involved in that stabbing. That's what all these fights are about. There may have been a bit of swaggering and someone got annoyed.'

Dizzee was taken straight to hospital after the attack and he told *Blender* that he spent his time there muttering about vengeance, saying 'Bastards', over and over. Dizzee also recalled the trauma to the *Daily Star*: 'It was all in slow motion. It was partly my fault. I got off my bike doing the bravery thing when I should have just sped off. But I don't like to walk away. I don't like to be picked on. Growing up where I did you learn to fight. Getting stabbed, it's not glamorous. It was a bad time. I had internal bleeding in my chest so I was coughing up blood all the time, I was on a drip that was getting on my nerves.'

Dizzee hasn't spoken much about the stabbing as he doesn't want to use it to shape his career, as other rappers have done. 'I didn't want to make a meal of getting stabbed. And 50 Cent had already done it. I didn't want to compete with getting shot nine times.' Not only is he not keen to talk to the media about the stabbing he was also not keen to talk to the police about it. After all, he isn't a snitch. 'I got a problem, I'm not going to the police,' says Dizzee. The police were desperate to talk to Dizzee

but he told them nothing. They also interviewed Megaman of So Solid Crew, but they got nothing from him either.

Two armed guards were placed outside Dizzee's room at the Naya Olympic private clinic as fears grew that the gang would return, but against doctor's orders, Dizzee discharged himself and moved to another hospital. Megaman insisted he didn't know who was involved and everything was cool between Roll Deep and the So Solid Crew.

Years later, in 2009, Dizzee gave his most revealing interview about the incident to the *Daily Mirror*, saying how he struggled initially to get any treatment on the island: 'They didn't want to treat me because I brought shame on to the island. But I got there and I got stabbed up the second night. I was new to the place. I didn't know anything about all this.'

When he discharged himself after three days – against the doctor's advice and still high on morphine – Dizzee's manager and producer Nick Cage got him into a hotel room, where he was able to mull over the incident. 'I was sitting there with the sea in front of me, just fucking sitting there for hours just staring at the sea, part feeling sorry for myself, part feeling very, very angry, part feeling just quite confused,' Dizzee remembers.

Reportedly he sank into a psychological hole, where he listened to the dark Streets track, 'Stay Positive', which must have given him some relief that there was light at the end of the tunnel. But he was in an awful way and just eating was a struggle: 'I was really weak,' Dizzee recalls. 'I kept walking the hotel corridors. I had to go and get food, this restaurant was only a quarter of a mile away but it felt like days away because I was so weak.'

It's almost irrelevant who did it, even though Dizzee must

know who it was – even if no one else quite does. He seems to have decided to chalk the whole incident up to experience – forget and move on. 'I did just take it like every other thing that's happened to me,' Dizzee told the *Guardian*. 'I've been through madnesses before, violence. You can't say you're from the street and talk shit if you haven't been through those kind of experiences… I know that was a big thing, but I've been through stuff.'

When Dizzee returned to his estate in Bow, where he was still living at the time, he was in a bad way both physically and mentally.

The day he got home the doctors re-stitched his wounds, but ever the pro he still went to work: 'The same day, I went to the studio and I was recording this track, "Respect Me", and it hurt when I was rapping, but I thought, "I've got to do this."'

The experience lent a darker edge to his music, which he is only just shedding. 'It changes you into a really dark person,' he says. 'But really, I'm a joker. I'm a clown. It's only just starting to come out in my music. All I really want to do is make people jump around and smile.'

Dizzee was used to adversity and facing dangerous situations by this stage in his life, but the stabbing helped refocus his mind away from the troubles that surrounded his type of music at the time. He knew that if he allowed all that ghetto nonsense to sidetrack him he'd never achieve his goals. 'Which near-death experience? I've had a few – car crashes, plus a few other sticky or violent situations,' Dizzee told the *Independent*. 'The most widely known was when I was stabbed in Ayia Napa. It made me a lot more focused; it made me wake up… I want people to like my music, so it made me work harder at that. Those news stories will die down; people will stop caring about them. But I don't want them to forget my music.'

That's not to say he doesn't still feel angry about what happened, and he certainly has no desire to return to Ayia Napa, as he told the *Daily Mirror*: 'Nothing would inspire me to go back there. It had a lasting effect. I've still got the scars and certain things will always trigger emotions.'

Back in the UK, after the stabbing the media went mad, hailing the So Solid/Roll Deep rift as the UK's equivalent of Biggie and Tupac. In reality, though, the situation was much tamer, with Megaman hushing rumours to the *Scotsman*: 'There ain't no story with me and Dizzee Rascal… me and Dizzee Rascal are cool. At the end of the day, there was a little disruption with a few other guys who was around us... It's all level now. I spoke to Dizzee and the whole of Roll Deep. They're cool with us. It's just one of those things.' And Megaman went on to say how he felt that 'Dizzee's well talented, man'.

Suffice to say Dizzee's response to hearing this was confusion, as he'd been used to getting nothing but abuse from So Solid's people. 'Yeah, yeah… I don't really care about them, to tell you the truth, but it's good that Megaman said that,' says Dizzee. 'That's why I don't really talk about So Solid – they can't make up their minds. They'll be saying we need to hook up, blah blah, the next, on a mix CD, this one's running their mouth, that one's running their mouth.'

One thing there was no confusion about in the aftermath of Ayia Napa was that, as well as his life, Dizzee's career was in the balance. If these ever-present petty feuds dragged him down, his career would be over before it had even begun. Nick

Cage had flown out to Ayia Napa as soon as he heard that Dizzee had been stabbed and rushed to his hospital bed to help him as best he could. 'I had to nurse him for a fortnight in this manky hotel,' Cage told the *Guardian*. 'The doctors were not nice to us, they refused to treat him... He had checked himself out of hospital when I got there. He was high on painkillers riding around on his moped, being pursued by tabloid journalists. I was like: wait until the painkillers wear off. I have lost three friends in these kinds of incidents – knifings. He was lucky.'

Dizzee will never forget Nick for being a solid friend and coming out to help him when he was in big trouble. 'Nick took me in as a kid,' Dizzee says. 'He could see that I was willing to go all out. So he went all out for me. We are family. We are from pretty much the same place... And he came and got me in Ayia Napa.'

Dizzee was eager to put this violent episode behind him and not turn it into a symbol of his fledgling career. Despite including a lot of violent themes in his early works, Dizzee had plenty more to talk about than a life of a crime and troubles. 'A lot of rap comes from inner cities where youths are exposed to that kind of thing and then rap about it,' he explains. 'Sure I saw gangs, guns and fighting, but I was just as influenced by girls and partying and having a good time.'

More than anything, though, Dizzee realised that he had a career and a life that he needed to preserve. It wasn't worth risking for these petty ego battles. 'I'm less likely to punch you in the face if you talk shit,' he admitted to the *Daily Mirror*. 'I've got a career to think about and you can't just go around punching people in the face. In society, there's rules and regulations. Just paying bills, rent... adult stuff helps you grow up.'

10

MERCURIAL RISE

The stabbing in Ayia Napa was a wake-up call for Dizzee. He knew that his career was on a knife-edge, and that the way in which he conducted himself over the coming months would have a lasting effect on his life. If he chose to get dragged down by all the other nonsense, there was every chance he'd end up dead or in prison. All around him there were talented kids throwing away their future to petty nonsense. He need only look at Crazy Titch – who ended up in prison a few years later – as an example of how easy it was to get dragged down by exactly the kind of conflict Dizzee was in. Dizzee needed to sort himself out and focus on his music, and that alone.

As he said years later to the *Daily Telegraph*, it was music that came to his rescue and became his form of recovery and rehabilitation from the stabbing: 'There's been a lot of reha-bilitation over the years,' he said. 'It's not like I went for counselling after getting stabbed, like most people would. I just kind of threw myself into my work and jumped into the public eye. I suppose from that perspective I'm quite lucky not to be strung out on heroin or something.'

Thankfully for Dizzee there was another major development in the summer of 2003, which helped focus his mind away from all the negativity surrounding the trouble in Ayia Napa. The Mercury Prize is awarded annually for the best album from the United Kingdom and Ireland. It was established by the British Phonographic Industry and British Association of Record Dealers in 1992 as an alternative to the Brit Awards, which many felt was too commercialised, and for music purists it's considered the most prestigious award in the industry.

Nominations are chosen by a selected panel of musicians, music executives, journalists and other figures in UK and Irish music industry. Previous winners had included ground-breaking acts such as Primal Scream, Suede, M People, Portishead, Pulp, Roni Size, Gomez, Talvin Singh, Badly Drawn Boy, PJ Harvey and Ms Dynamite, and from that list Talvin Singh had blazed a trail for East London.

At about the same time that Dizzee returned from Ayia Napa and was having his stitches checked out by a local doctor, he heard that *Boy in da Corner* had been nominated for the Mercury Prize. He was the first underground grime artist to receive such acknowledgement. Seeing as the album had only just been released, it was an amazing achievement for it to be in the running for the most sought-after award in the industry within weeks. Also nominated in 2003 were Athlete – *Vehicles & Animals*, Eliza Carthy – *Anglicana*, Coldplay – *A Rush of*

Blood to the Head, The Darkness – *Permission to Land*, Floetry – *Floetic*, Soweto Kinch – *Conversations With the Unseen*, Lemon Jelly – *Lost Horizons*, The Thrills – *So Much for the City*, Martina Topley-Bird – *Quixotic*, Radiohead – *Hail to the Thief*, and Terri Walker – *Untitled*.

For Dizzee this was all new territory, which he wasn't too sure of. 'When I got told I was nominated, I was like "… Mercury… Mercury Awards…" I weren't too sure what it was,' Dizzee admitted to the *Scotsman*. 'I knew that Dynamite won, I knew it was a massive thing in the industry. When I actually got there, I looked around and thought, Am I really meant to be here?'

Obviously Coldplay and Radiohead were the biggest names on the list, but the prize had a habit of being awarded to more unknown names over the years, so people weren't certain that it would go to either of the big guns. Many people were tipping The Darkness to win, and if truth be told, Dizzee was a bit of an outsider. Although not for Nick Hasted of the *Independent*, who said at the time of Dizzee's nomination that 'the debut album of eighteen-year-old Dizzee Rascal has just been nominated for the Mercury Music Prize, but more important is the impact it makes on your head as it forces its way up from the underground – musical and social… If it wins the Mercury, and becomes the middle class's annual "street" purchase, a million dinner parties will grind to a halt.'

There was certainly a fever on the streets regarding Dizzee's new album, but many doubted whether its rough-and-ready sound would be acknowledged by the mainstream. In July *Tiscali Music News* said, 'That this album will win prizes is beyond doubt, although it remains to be seen whether those who aren't used to the real sound of the underground will have the breadth of mind to embrace the Dizzee man.

'However the gauntlet is on the ground and it was Dizzee Rascal and "The Boys in da Corner" set who threw it there. Not just album of the next century, but of the century after as well.'

On the night of Tuesday 8 September 2003, Dizzee arrived at the swanky Grosvenor House Hotel for the awards. He couldn't quite believe he was there and he certainly didn't expect to win. He found everything so bemusing that he arrived wearing question marks all over his jeans. Nonetheless he decided to tuck into the free champagne and at least have fun. When his name was called out, it was said in the *Scotsman* that 'Dizzee's "natural reaction" – possibly conditioned by years of having his name shouted out by teachers and authority figures – was to stand up'.

'I didn't really know what was going on,' recalls Dizzee. 'I accepted it, I was happy, I was drunk. But over the moon? That didn't sink in for weeks.' When he received his award from the previous year's winner, Ms Dynamite, he said in his acceptance speech, 'I want to thank God, my mum and my family and everyone in the underground. Remember to support British talent – because it is there.' For Dizzee this was an award for the underground as much as it was for him and he wanted to make sure that where he came from got some recognition. 'I come from nothing – I come from the underground, pirate radio stations, I come from the ground, man.'

At the time Dizzee had no idea what the award meant – or would go on to mean in the future – telling *GQ* a few years later, 'I didn't really have a reference for the Mercury before

Dynamite won it, so I just kind of got on with shit. I had my own issues as well that I had to prove that I could still do it. I just know the coverage I got through winning the Mercury Prize, it was ridiculous. The whole world wanted to know about it.'

Dizzee, aged just seventeen and eleven months, was the youngest ever winner of the Mercury Prize and only the second rapper, after Ms Dynamite, to take the award home. From that day on Dizzee's career would never be the same. The following morning he woke to find the ever-intrusive British media camped outside his mum's house in Bow. Suddenly everyone wanted to know who this young star was.

Dizzee's publicist from XL told the *Guardian* about the media scrum: 'The press are outside his house. I think they want to talk to his mum. His brain's a bit scrambled at the moment.' Speaking the day after receiving the award, Dizzee told how he'd felt completely shocked by the award and what it meant to everyone: 'I didn't expect it to get this much coverage, because it's grimy and the kind of audience it was aimed for isn't a massive audience. I always put people with my kind of background first. It's just amazing that it's reached so many people.'

It wasn't just a big night for Dizzee, it was a big night for everyone who'd supported him, from his mother to Nick Cage to his old school teacher Tim Smith. It was also massive for his label XL, in particular Nick Huggett, who was the A&R man who'd signed the teenager after hearing his white label 'I Luv U' on a pirate radio station. He later talked to the *Observer* about discovering Dizzee: 'I was struck because it was the first time I'd heard someone rap with a cockney accent and the music he was rapping over was like nothing I'd heard before. He was the artist and he won it [the Mercury Prize], but I felt like I had some input and ultimately I just felt really proud. Especially because of the kind of music that it is – it's not commercial or mainstream. It's not the sort of thing you expect to win awards, as much as you love it.'

One person who wasn't with Dizzee when he won the Mercury was his old partner, Wiley. Despite not being there to celebrate Dizzee's success, Wiley was still supportive of his old partner in the media, telling *Jockey Slut* magazine how proud he was of Dizzee: 'That was good [winning Mercury]. Dizzee is big and there is no limits to what he can get, win or how much he can sell. Me and him we got signed together and we got signed for the same reason, both because we produce, we are artists and we were big in the underground. I'm behind him. My spirit is with him, his spirit is with me. We just do what we're doing. Even though we're not together, we're still trying to do the same thing but we're just different people. He's trying to go out into the world and let everyone know, and so am I. I don't chase him around and following. I wait till I go in the world and we'll see each other.'

According to his label Dizzee had to 'go to ground' after the award. The media were after anything they could get and XL were keen to keep Dizzee focused on his music and nothing else. Six weeks later, he emerged and told the *Scotsman*, 'You can't argue with the paparazzi, man.'

But still Dizzee kept a cool head and stayed humble and true to himself. 'I don't really class myself as a musician, I can make music but I'm not the greatest technically. There were other people who were technically better than me in school but I knew how I wanted to sound and all I needed was to work out how to do it. For the past four years I have been focused on my music: DJing, doing pirate radio, playing at little raves and youth clubs before making the album.'

Now that Dizzee had made it he knew he had to keep out of trouble for the first time in his life if he was going to have a future from here on. 'I have had the odd little moment,' he told the *Daily Telegraph*. 'But on the whole I do a pretty good job of holding things together.'

Dizzee had been in the news all summer because of the stabbing on Ayia Napa, but now at last he was getting mainstream media attention for his talents. The day after the award Dizzee listened to the news discuss what he would do with his future after winning the Mercury. 'Shit, man. They're discussing my future on the BBC. All these people talking, talking about me. I'm just like – carry on. News, innit?'

A lot of the talk during the aftermath of the awards ceremony was about the 'curse of the Mercury Prize'. It was widely noted that many of the previous winners had gone on to have plenty of immediate success after winning the award only to vanish into music history, and many were predicting that Dizzee would be yesterday's news by Christmas. It was a very valid argument when you looked at the previous winners.

Things went downhill immediately for the original winners, Primal Scream, who lost the actual award and the £20,000 cheque when out celebrating the same night. Their follow-up album wasn't as well received and they've struggled to make commercial inroads since. The 1993 winners, Suede, also found it hard to capitalise on their success. Perfectly poised to lead the Britpop revolution, their follow-up album, *Dog Man Star,* was a let-down. They then lost guitarist (arguably the band's primary musical force) Bernard Butler following a bust-up and were never quite the same again.

M People's *Elegant Slumming* controversially took the award in 1994 over Blur's *Parklife* and The Prodigy's *Music for the Jilted Generation*. But their follow-up work failed to impress, except for a surprise comeback in 1998 with the single 'Angel St'. Lead singer Heather Small released a solo album in 2000, but there has been very little from any of the band since then. Portishead followed up the success of *Dummy*, winning the 1995 award with a critically acclaimed self-titled second album two years later, but haven't made the same impact since.

Despite Jarvis Cocker remaining in the public eye after winning the 1996 Mercury Prize, Pulp never quite managed to repeat the highs of their award-winning album *Different Class*. And the same could be said for Roni Size, who never made an album reaching the Reprazent's 97 Mercury Prize-winning standards. The parallels were already being drawn between the two underground artists and it was felt that Dizzee would follow Roni Size's path more than anyone else.

1998 winners Gomez were as little-known as Dizzee when they won. Just a bunch of students from Southport, winning the award exploded their career. They had a decent follow-up album in *Liquid Skin,* but overexposure (in part due to the Mercury Award) proved to be their downfall and the band have mainly pursued solo projects since their early-millennium heyday.

Fellow East Londoner Talvin Singh made waves in 1999 with his bangrha/drum and bass fusion. But after winning the award both his follow-up albums failed to make headway in the charts and Singh moved more into the production side of the industry.

Badly Drawn Boy did manage to break the curse after winning in 2000 and going on to release a couple of successful albums and the movie soundtrack to *About a Boy*.

PJ Harvey already had a well-established career when she won in 2001, which makes it difficult to compare her to Dizzee, but Ms Dynamite was a comparison that many commentators were drawing. Coming from the garage scene, she was the darling of UK urban music at the time, but still her career didn't go on to much greater heights in terms of huge commercial success after winning the award.

It seemed as though the writing was on the wall for Dizzee. So he should enjoy the flash of success that surrounded winning the award and milk the moment for all it was worth because, if history was anything to go by, he'd be yesterday's news within a couple of years.

Suddenly Dizzee was a commercial name, which could potentially leave him in no-man's land – too underground for the mainstream and too mainstream for the underground. Was he worried about losing credibility with the scene he'd come from, as some said had happened with The Streets after Mike Skinner's success? Apparently not. When talking to the *Independent* he said, 'I've got nothing but respect for Mike Skinner – even though I called him Frank Skinner by mistake once. But he shouldn't worry about that [losing respect], because progression is progression, and if garage people decide they don't like ya, that fanbase ain't that big anyway. He's progressed to the middle classes, to make people understand him, but garage people still know who he is. It's the same with me. I ain't worried about, oh, they're gonna think I'm not ghetto no more.'

For Dizzee it looked like his days in the poverty-stricken estates of East London were behind him. While it was time for him to move on, though, he could never forget where he came from – he would carry the streets with him for ever. 'Street's with you for ever. It's good, if you apply it to something else. It don't do much for you otherwise. I might never be socially accepted, or middle class, but you make your own straps when you're from the road. I ain't got nothing against middle- or upper-class people. I just ain't got much in common with them. I think it's more important to come from nothing and make yourself big. No disrespect to anyone born with a silver spoon in their mouth. I was born in this little bit of rock in the East End. But I'm in the world now.'

Dizzee had achieved a great deal in a very short time and he was still only just eighteen years old, but when asked at the time by the *Independent* if he was happy with his achievements he replied, 'Yeah, man. I'm alive for a start, innit? Some people, they go to sleep, and don't ever wake up.'

Sales of *Boy in da Corner* began to rocket after the Mercury Prize. And if they hadn't been praising it before, soon every publication in the country had jumped on the bandwagon and was singing from the roof tops about Dizzee's debut album. For the most part, the media were obsessed with the insight the CD gave them into the mind of a disaffected inner-city youth. And through Dizzee's music what they saw was anger. Alexis Petridis wrote, 'On *Boy in da Corner*, Mills' own persona is about as far removed from the standard alpha male rapper as it is possible to get: instead, he is riven with anger and despair and occasionally suicidal.'

Once success started to make an impression on young

Dizzee, he began to lose a lot of that anger. 'Do I still feel like that now? Every now and then,' Dizzee told Petridis. 'However I feel at the time will come out in my music. It doesn't necessarily have to be angry. Right now I'm feeling quite happy. I'm not angry about too much right now, man.'

With a fresh outlook on life it was time for Dizzee to make some headway into the singles chart after the modest success of his first release, 'I Luv U'.

'Fix Up, Look Sharp' was released in August 2003, just before his Mercury success, and peaked at number 17, buoyed up by an artsy video that was filmed on Dizzee's first trip to LA. 'LA is nang,' he later told *Blender*. 'Before *Boy in da Corner* was released I hadn't left Britain,' Dizzee told the *Independent*. 'The first time I travelled was when I went to shoot my second video in Los Angeles.'

Dizzee's first professional move post-Mercury was to release 'Jus' a Rascal', which peaked at number 30. Along with 'Fix Up, Look Sharp', 'Jus' a Rascal' was used in an episode of cult hit TV show *Skins,* as well as in the film *Kidulthood*. The film – a gritty drama about the troubles facing youths in inner-city London – was the movie equivalent of Dizzee's album, except it was set in West not East London. Much like *Boy in da Corner*, the film deals with issues such as teen pregnancy, violence, ego, poverty and suicide, and the *Daily Mirror* described it as being 'as potent as a shot of vodka before breakfast – a harrowing, uncompromisingly bleak but thoughtful look at the anguish of being young and poor in Britain.'

Like Dizzee Rascal's music, the critics lapped up this raw cinematic view of London, which for once wasn't seen through the eyes of Hugh Grant or Richard Curtis, but through the eyes of inner-city kids. The film has the same irreverent humour as Dizzee's music. The *Guardian*'s Miranda Sawyer called the film 'a rollicking UK youth ride, cinematically filmed, persuasively acted and bumped along by a fantastic all-British soundtrack… It's also very funny, laced with a humour of the slapped-in-the-face-with-a-kipper sort: you can't help laughing because it's so outrageous.'

Kidulthood was just another part of London's underground scene, alongside Dizzee Rascal's *Boy in da Corner,* and was part of the multimedia London ghetto movement that was being displayed to the wider world.

London was the star of Dizzee's next music video for his third single, 'Jus' a Rascal', which shows Dizzee in a familiar environment – with his mates partying on a boat under London Bridge. The video also sees the first appearance of future star Tinchy Stryder. Dizzee had known Tinchy since their days growing up in Bow. Dizzee was just a year older than Tinchy and, like Diz, Tinchy had been a music hustler from a young age. Starting out on pirate radio in East London at the age of fourteen, he got to know Wiley and Dizzee there. He later joined the Roll Deep crew and gained his stage name 'Tinchy' because of his short height, 5 foot 1 inch. He's since gone on to forge a successful solo career that's still running, becoming yet another graduate from the Bow-based Roll Deep musical academy.

Given that Dizzee was the man of the moment at the time, everybody was desperate to collaborate with him. First in the queue, though, was Basement Jaxx, a house music duo signed to the same label, XL. Dizzee collaborated on their track 'Lucky

Star', showing early signs of the diversity he's now famous for. The track reached number 23 in the charts and was another hit to add to his growing repertoire.

11

COMING TO AMERICA

By the Christmas of 2003, Dizzee could reflect on a crazy year. His world had been turned upside down, going from ghetto no-hoper to the golden boy of the music biz. He'd spent most of the year churning out tracks, but now it was time for the world to see his live show. Dizzee continued his upwardly mobile momentum by heading Stateside, where he performed a couple of shows to promote his album, which had just been released to an American audience.

In the US the initial media reaction to *Boy in da Corner* is best described as positively bewildered, in that they liked him but weren't sure where to place him. Sasha Frere-Jones wrote in *Slate* online magazine in January 2004, 'He seems a contender for permanently well-known unknown in the States, because his abrasive, energetic music doesn't fit easily in any American genre. That doesn't mean he's not an MC – just that there's no easy and quick way for Americans to understand exactly what kind of MC he is.'

The obvious comparisons Stateside were with their own breed of black urban artists. But to do this would be to miss much of the point of Dizzee, as Sasha Frere-Jones appreciated: '50 Cent sounds like Simon and Garfunkel next to Dizzee Rascal.'

American bloggers were quick to latch on to Dizzee, praising him for establishing a new genre, *British* hip-hop. It was a good point, as up until now most British rap was just an imitation of the American version. The same could not be said of *Boy in da Corner*.

Matthew Pollesel wrote in *Splendid* magazine, 'There's a reason Dizzee Rascal's debut beat out Radiohead, Coldplay, The Darkness and others to win the Mercury Music Prize last summer. It won because it's the sound of British hip-hop being born as a distinct genre, completely separate from the American strain. Where others have merely hinted at that evolution, *Boy in da Corner* is a bold proclamation... If *Boy in da Corner* marks the beginning of distinctly British hip-hop, the genre's standards are already impressively high.'

Dizzee arrived for his first US gig in April 2004. The day before the gig he met William Shaw of *Blender*, who noted how jet-lagged he looked. 'My body clock is effed,' Dizzee said. 'It has been for about three years. I don't know when I'm supposed to sleep.' Nobody was sure about how the States would receive the very British Dizzee Rascal, but respected *Blender* magazine was quite open to the young upstart: 'Post-Slick Rick, it has been almost impossible to imagine hip-hop with a British accent. But here's an MC who rhymes crew with the quintessentially English boast that he's "flushing MCs down the loo". The Streets' Mike Skinner made inroads with *Original Pirate Material*, but Dizzee is something else.'

Dizzee's first US gig was in New York's Hipster HQ, Williamsburg, where US online magazine *Dusted* pitched up to check out the latest UK pretender to the US hip-hop scene: 'Given the relative monotony of American commercial hip-hop radio, one would have to wonder if a kid from the streets of London with a rubbery British accent would have even half a chance of competing against the likes of the Family Roc or Lil Jon's ever-expanding clique. However, based upon his debut American performance at a new club called Volume in the hipster enclave of Williamsburg, one would be inclined to think that the spins are his for the taking.'

Under the vaulted ceilings and brash white walls of newly opened club Volume, Dizzee found himself in the kind of bare industrial space he was used to performing in during his rave days. Oddly, there was no stage in either of the spaces' two rooms, leaving Dizzee to traipse around the floor with his audience. It wasn't too different to his youth-club gigs, except for the resident eighteen-wheeler flatbed truck he could use to jump around on.

Before Dizzee played, various DJs spun through familiar American and Jamaican tracks, Lex's Tes warmed up the crowd in the smaller space before the main event, and when Dizzee bowled onto the truck, the New York crowd erupted. By all accounts he was quite nervous playing in such alien surroundings, but ever the performer, he leapt onto the stage in front of his first American audience and proclaimed, 'We're bringing London to you. LDN to the NYC!' Then opened with

'I Luv U', hyping the crowd and stalking about the stage as revellers' hands remained in the air.

He stuck mostly to material from *Boy in da Corner*, bellowing out his biggest hits, 'Stop Dat' and the crowd-pleasing 'Fix Up, Look Sharp'. The US crowd loved it. Hyped-up, Dizzee wowed the crowed by peppering his set with a few freestyle a capellas, just to show off his amazing freestyle abilities. He had a mishap, however, during 'Brand New Day' when the record began skipping. Unfazed and ever the professional, Dizzee instructed the DJ to cut the record and proceeded to finish the song without music.

The US crowd seemed to love Dizzee's fresh new take on a genre they consider very much their own. *Dusted* said: 'In this era of shiny MCs and constant rhymes about jewellery and clothes, such an introspective voice proved increasingly welcome throughout the course of the evening... Dizzy [sic] Rascal had fuelled the crowd's energy with his grimy sound-scapes... It remains to be seen whether Dizzy Rascal will scale the heights of fame in this country that he's already navigated in his own, but with a tour in the works for this summer, people should have ample opportunity to evaluate the hype themselves.' Dizzee was still very much a small fish in the American pond, but he was certainly making friends.

American musicians in the hip-hop scene started sitting up and taking notice, too. One of the godfathers of rap, the late great Guru, was a Dizzee fan, saying of 'Fix Up, Look Sharp', 'That's like ragga mixed with hip-hop with an incredible, orig-inal UK style. I honestly believe he can sell mad records in the States. He's got good energy, man.'

Upon hearing this praise, Dizzee beamed to *Blender*, 'Coming from Guru? The essence of old-school hip-hop? The real innovator? He's a pioneer.'

Two days after his first US gig, Dizzee flew out to Los Angeles for his American TV debut, appearing on ABC's prime-time chat show *Jimmy Kimmel Live!* Before the show he spent time driving around LA listening to local hip-hop and shopping. He stayed in the ultra-trendy Standard Hotel on Hollywood Boulevard with his manager Nick Cage and DJ Slimzee. Before rehearsals Dizzee went to JMartin Designs on Melrose Avenue. JMartin custom paints clothing for Method Man, Xzibit, Jennifer Lopez and David Beckham. Dizzee commissioned a jumpsuit with a spray-painted portrait on the front, plus his personal logo – a dog turd surrounded by buzzing flies – which he wanted for the following year's Brit Awards.

The following day Dizzee went through a rehearsal of his performance on Jimmy Kimmel. After the run-through, the show's floor manager approached Dizzee to warn him that he was flashing three inches of arse crack. Apparently that was going to be too much for the American audience.

That night, just before the performance went live, Jimmy Kimmel showed a still from the rehearsal: three inches of Dizzee's arse crack, pixelated to avoid offending more sensitive viewers.

Jimmy introduced Dizzee to millions of American viewers as, 'The man standing next to me just beat out Coldplay and Radiohead to win the Mercury Prize for best British album of the year... from a little town called London, Dizzee Rascal, everybody!'

Dizzee, in turn, alluded to his bum being shown on television when he announced, 'We're dead serious, we didn't come to make an arse of ourselves', before launching into a wildly energized performance of 'Fix Up, Look Sharp'. Afterwards, when was asked about the incident he replied, 'Everything comes with a price. I'll be honest, I thought my arse was blacker than that.' It was the first time the general US public had got to see Dizzee Rascal and he wouldn't be forgotten in a hurry. Years later he referred to the incident when the *Guardian* asked him what his most embarrassing moment ever was: 'On *Jimmy Kimmel Live!* in Hollywood. They showed me doing my rehearsal and my trousers fell down. That day I didn't wear no underwear, and you could see my bare arse.'

A few months later, in the summer of 2004, Dizzee returned to the US to play the Irving Plaza for two nights with his label-mate The Streets at the 2,000-capacity venue – tickets sold out in no time. The venue is renowned for being a discovery-venue for all the latest indie acts, which made for an interesting crowd. As *NME* put it, 'Tonight the place stinks of cheap perfume worn by chicks ordering Malibu and Diet Coke and letting their backwards-cap-sporting boyfriends pay for it. And that's not all. We've also got prim sixteen-year-old girls making eyes at dangerous-looking guys in basketball jerseys posed with arms across their chests, looking sceptically at geeky indie-rockers nervously chewing the straws of their cocktails.' This was a far cry from the East London rude boys he was used to playing to, but Dizzee was happy to run with the oddball crowd and blow the roof off the venue.

Dizzee marched onstage wearing a Yankees' cap, gleaming white sneakers and a pair of blue jeans decorated with a thick white stripe on the rear. The crowd recognised the look, with the cap, trainers and bling, but they couldn't quite recognise the 'rapid stream of incomprehensible words that came tumbling out'. Either way the audience roared and went crazy for his twisted new sound. As *NME* put it, 'This crowd may be an odd cross-section of freaks and geeks, but they have two things in common: they have absolutely no idea what the fuck Dizzee Rascal is saying, and they completely adore every last word.'

Dizzee churned out hits like 'Vexed', 'Jus' A Rascal' and 'Fix Up, Look Sharp', and it just got better and better throughout the night, with everyone adoring the kid from Bow.

'Dizzee's set feels like a gracefully played game of musical pinball, all spliced and split analogue sounds overlaid by perfectly serrated rhymes. The audience is like a cult of willing acolytes. They sing his songs for him when he offers them the mic. They bob their heads at his command. He points to the balcony and everyone screams, he points to the pit and everyone screams louder, he grins and turns his cap sideways... everyone screams themselves hoarse... tonight it's Dizzee Rascal who brings that brilliance alive onstage.'

Save for his early raves and the odd supporting role, such as Jay-Z's gig, the UK mainstream hadn't seen much of Dizzee live. In 2004 that would all change when he was invited to play London's Royal Festival Hall. It was a breakthrough moment for Dizzee to be invited to play the prestigious a 2,900-seat venue within London's Southbank Centre, and it was a far cry from his days playing the 'gutter raves'.

According to *Contact Music*, 'Worlds collided when the ghetto street sounds of Dizzee Rascal's crew played a venue normally accustomed to more reserved performances from classical musicians.' Dizzee brought a street atmosphere to the stage with bold red and black lighting and a cold blue floor, and opened with one of his favourite tracks, 'Sittin' Here'. He then stood up, greeted 'the L–D–N' and proceeded to get the slightly reserved crowd on to their feet, proclaiming, 'This ain't no sit-down thing.' He asked the audience to 'listen faster', then he blew them away with his machine-gun rap, creating a fever of frenzied excitement. Dizzee played a few more tracks from *Boy in da Corner* before attempting to bring things up a notch with some audience participation. The thoroughly middle-class crowd weren't quite as enthusiastic in parts as Dizzee would have like, though, and at one point he hollered, 'You people are gonna respect me if it kills me.'

According to Contact Music, 'Dizzee rewarded obliging fans at the front by gracing their outstretched hands with his, but this atmosphere struggled to spread through the whole auditorium. It was not designed for that.' It was the first time Dizzee had come into close contact with his more mainstream, middle-class fanbase, and he needed to learn how to play the crowd. By the time he came out for his encore, though, they were in a frenzy for him. The audience went mad for the hit single 'Fix Up, Look Sharp', and from then on Dizzee knew that it would be his more experimental music that would hold the greatest appeal.

Some people weren't convinced that Dizzee's act suited such mainstream arenas. Alex Mula of Contact Music commented, 'His powerful lyrics appeal to all kids, ghetto or not, and this was reflected in the culturally diverse audience. But Dizzee belongs to the street and he's proud of it. His razor-sharp tongue sounded out of place in an arena used to hearing orchestras play. That he was invited to play at the Royal Festival Hall at all is testament to his award-winning talent. Dizzee is a fantastic performer but homogeny breeds mediocrity and he should be seen in a venue with a character matching his own.'

But Dizzee went on to show that he could hold any audience on any stage, be it the Brit Awards, Glastonbury or the Royal Albert Hall.

12

SHOWTIME

Ever the workaholic, Dizzee wasted no time in getting into the studio to make a second album. This time, thanks to his success, the album was made with a few more gadgets than his school computers and the turntables his mum bought him. They say your second album is the most important one you ever make, especially for Mercury winners, with their history of flunking after their initial success.

Any doubts people had about Dizzee's musical direction were quashed when 'Stand Up Tall' was released on 23 August 2004. It rocketed up the charts to number 10, making it Dizzee's first top-10 hit. The up-tempo track was slightly more polished than his previous recordings. Over a standard fast beat, Dizzee uses a simple, three-note synth hook that sounds like it's been taken from an old games console. During the verses it becomes a frenetic, two-note baseline that punctuates

Dizzee's distinctive vocal cadence. Then, when the chorus comes along, he injects a second fantastic synth hook and the melodic keyboard juts in, offsetting the song's gritty, urgent sound perfectly.

On Dizzee's insistence, he flew out to the US again to shoot the video. There might be a London taxi in the video, but it was actually shot in Atlanta, apparently because of its reputation as the strip-joint capital of the States. Dizzee and the director wanted lots of pretty scantily clad girls in the video and, no doubt, to have a little off-set fun.

The 'Stand Up Tall' single was released on two CDs. The first featured the title track and 'Give U More', which would be the first time we'd see Dizzee work with his East London friend, D Double E of Newham Generals, who'd also worked with The Streets and Lethal Bizzle. Five different versions of 'Stand Up Tall' would be used on the second CD and the track would also feature on the EA Sports' video game, FIFA Street and in the 2005 film *The 40-Year-Old Virgin*, starring Steve Carrel. The *Guardian* reviewed the track as 'witty, knowing, and swaggering like Godzilla... over a pinging computer arcade synth riff.'

Dizzee's follow-up album, *Showtime*, was always going to be fascinating, and everyone involved in music was keen to see what he would do next. How would he follow up one of the most highly praised albums of the decade? The media was full of chatter about how second albums have been the graveyard of many a musician's career, but they've also been the making of some of the greats. 'The precedents for *Showtime* include Eminem's *The Marshall Mathers LP* and Tricky's spotlight-dodging second album, *Pre-Millennium Tension*,' said the

Guardian. Both were recorded quickly and came with cockily self-referential singles: 'The Real Slim Shady' and 'Tricky Kid'. However, whilst Eminem is still a massive star and household name, Tricky isn't.

The quality of *Showtime* would dictate which way Dizzee's career would go. The pressure was on and Dizzee knew it. After cramming a lifetime's work and ambition into a single record, the next one was a totally different proposition, and the pressure to exceed expectations and build upon his early success was immensely high. Dizzee had written most of his new songs while still promoting *Boy in da Corner*, with many songs being composed on the road, instead of at home. Now that he had found success, his time was far more precious and opportunities to work alone were considerably harder to come by.

Dizzee had also gone through a major lifestyle change in the past twelve months. He was no longer the boy in the corner, his talent had pushed him right into the spotlight and he was now viewed as the saviour of British urban music. One of the main draws of his first album was its raw autobiographical nature, but Dizzee wasn't living that edgy life any more. Instead of writing songs about trying to get out of the ghetto he'd grown up in, Dizzee had to write about what it was like now that he was out.

When you become famous all you have to write about is celebrity, money and sex, which had been done to death. Some artists, such as Jay-Z and Eminem, have excelled at that kind of songwriting, but Dizzee realized he would have to do something different on his second album if he was going to set himself apart. As Dorian Lynskey said in the *Guardian*, 'An MC's debut album is often fuelled by a lifetime of poverty and frustration, so sudden success creates a lyrical quandary… there are only two options: embrace success or rail against it. Jay-Z has recorded several albums of which the gist is, "I'm brilliant. Look at my new watch. It's got diamonds on it." Eminem, meanwhile, refined "be careful what you wish for" to a fine art.'

With *Boy in da Corner*, Dizzee Rascal had flipped UK hip-hop/garage/grime and British pop music completely on its head. He'd introduced the gritty side of London's East End garage scene to the rest of the world, which in the past year had proved to be the source of easily the most thrilling new music in the UK. To his credit, Dizzee headed straight back into the studio, and just over a year after the release of *Boy in da Corner* and, even more overwhelming to American fans, a mere eight months after its US release, he dropped the brashly titled *Showtime* on the world. It not only proved to be a worthy follow-up, it helped confirm how gifted he is. As the *Guardian* stated, 'The Bow teenager behind the churning anxiety of *Boy in da Corner*, last year's Mercury-winning debut, was never likely to kick back and enjoy the free trainers, but nor does he treat selling 250,000 albums and reaping blanket critical acclaim as some calamitous misfortune. So the title of *Showtime* is deeply ambivalent: both a triumphant throwdown and a sardonic dig at his newfound status.'

Before the album's release, rumours were flying about what direction Dizzee would take. The word amongst some folk was that he would work with an acclaimed American producer such as Kanye West. Most people saw this as a dodgy call, fearful that he'd become just another American wannabe and lose the East London essence that makes him unique. Thankfully, those fears were quelled. Musically, *Showtime* continues where *Boy in da Corner* left off, delivering more of those twisted, stuttering, hyperkinetic beats. But instead of the rough, raw, minimal arrangement, the sound on *Showtime* is much more dense, complete and varied. 'Though Dizzee's laptop dystopias are no longer shockingly new, they are ceaselessly ingenious.'

As ever, Dizzee uses all forms of musical influences to create his album: dancehall, electro, pop, African percussion and even some Asian influences. The most notable difference on the new album is that the beats are accompanied by more melodic rhythms. That and the fact that it's an all-together happier album, largely because Dizzee appears to be in a happier place.

Lyrically, Dizzee has progressed on this album, too. Overall, the tone is less gritty as Dizzee muses about the price of fame, and whether or not he can stay true to himself as his wealth and fame increases. His anger and intensity are replaced by humility and cheeky humour. While *Showtime* may not be as intense and close to the bone as the last album, it does have its share of edgy moments, which are best exemplified in 'Hype Talk', 'Face' and 'Respect Me'. Over the hard, glitchy, computerised beat in 'Hype Talk', Dizzee refers to himself in the third person and talks of the rumours surrounding the Ayia Napa stabbing and his subsequent estrangement from Wiley.

On the dark and heavy 'Face', he chats about the rivalries among his London peers, only to end the song with a self-deprecating soundbite featuring two young ladies questioning Dizzee's legitimacy and opting to listen to Jay-Z instead. The album peaks with 'Respect Me', which he recorded the day after he got back from Ayia Napa. In it Dizzee expresses his frustration at all his detractors, sneering, 'So many claims and no evidence… You people are gonna respect me if it kills you.'

For some, though, Dizzee's obsession with petty disputes is a let-down. 'Too often, he dwells on internecine squabbles of which the average listener knows, and cares, little,' said the *Guardian*. 'Compared with the evocative tower-block angst of "Get By" or "Graftin'", this recurring obsession with insular scene politics is a blind alley.' But in reality Dizzee was still strongly connected to the streets, which he hadn't fully escaped yet, and as a result some elements of *Showtime* reflect this.

Showtime picks up in the second half and really climaxes towards the end, creating some of Dizzee's best music so far. He'd already shown how he could transform an eighties pop/ rock anthem in *Boy in da Corner*'s 'Fix Up, Look Sharp', and he performs a similar trick on the astonishing track, 'Dream', where he takes 'Happy Talk', the silly 1982 Rodgers and Hammerstein cover by former Damned guitarist Captain Sensible, and uses it as the central hook in his own tale of the making of *Boy in da Corner*.

'The more challenging it got the more I fought it… Made an album, over 100,000 people bought it… thank you.' Dizzee shows his love for the ladies in the lecherous track, 'Girls', where Dizzee and guest Marga Man admiring ladies' assets through their rap.

The album climaxes with two excellent tracks, 'Imagine' and 'Fickle', where Dizzee takes a few steps back and analyses where he is and where he's come from. He uses gentle synth harmonies in 'Imagine' as he questions how his life would have been different if he'd grown up away from the estates, and wonders whether he'll be better off living away from all the crime in the city and whether people from the hood would call him a sell-out.

The dramatic 'Fickle' boasts Dizzee's incredible studio work, with a tense keyboard melody and uncharacteristically busy production. Lyrically, Dizzee raps directly and unapologetically.

If the aim of *Boy in da Corner* was to tell the wider world about the London ghetto, then the aim of *Showtime* was to say that Dizzee wasn't going to forget where he came from: 'I'm from the LDN, no forgettin' that, and the big UK I stay reppin' that,' says Dizzee at one point on *Showtime*. He also maintains a very socially conscious outlook on the new album, particularly with the message on the inner sleeve that states, 'Black Britain stop dying!' When asked about this in the *Observer* Dizzee comments on black violence in London during that period, stating how common it is: 'It's normal, the everyday shit I knew growing up. There was another one the other day – on All Saints train station in Poplar. Two kids were fighting, and one punched the other and knocked him down onto the train track...'

In *Showtime*, Dizzee evolves but stays fiercely loyal to his roots, and the album was, largely, as well received as *Boy in da Corner*. At times he comes across as brash and comically brutal: 'I ain't mad, I'm a lovely lad, I'll give you the loveliest beatin' that you ever had.' But underneath all the self-hype and attitude it's the exposed vulnerable side that once more made Dizzee so appealing.

The media threw their hands up in high praise of Dizzee's second coming, claiming that it only confirmed the hype surrounding the young star. However, already questions were being asked about where he'd go from here: 'That Dizzee is the most dextrous and quotable MC Britain has ever produced is beyond dispute, but any rapper, however gifted, needs something to rap about, and the trials of fame offer diminishing returns. Dizzee might want to consider how Eminem and Tricky handled their third albums. One accepted his new position and learned to master it, at the cost of his abrasive edge; the other descended into self-immolating paranoia until all but the most hardcore fans had fled weeping. A problem for Dizzee's next album, then. For now, at least, there's no stopping him.'

Showtime was always going to suffer through comparison with Dizzee's all-conquering debut, and many critics claimed it wasn't quite as good. 'The result is an album I'm more likely to hold out tentatively to a few friends than aggressively push on everyone I talk to,' says Gavin Mueller of *Stylus*. But the quality of his work was undisputed, with critics claiming that *Showtime* had put to bed any feeling that he was a 'flash in the pan': 'Needless to say, the novelty status once accorded to this maverick by short-sighted cynics has now been obliterated by a shower of genius juice,' said Andy Kellman of *All Music*.

Initially *Showtime* seemed to be a bigger success than *Boy in da Corner* when it entered the UK albums chart at number 8, but in the US sales were massively down to around 16,000 copies, a big decline on the 58,000 his debut sold. According to some US critics, Dizzee was 'hip-hop but of the fish-and-chips variety.' But there was still no doubting his musical skills, Stateside, they just weren't sure where or how to categorise him. 'If Dizzee misses on mainstream American airtime, it won't be for a lack of talent,' said Ben Yaster of *Dusted*. 'The more likely culprits are mainstream DJs who just don't know how to translate and mix Dizzee's lo-fi hyperspeak. For sure,

"Stand Up Tall" and *Showtime* sound foreign, but not because Dizzee Rascal doesn't know how to steer hip-hop's wagon. He just drives it on the different side of the road.'

A large part of the problem in the US was that Dizzee was being pigeonholed as a rap musician, which would, in turn, confuse many of the listeners. As *Rep Reviews* says, 'This is not rap music. I have observed that most people approach Dizzee Rascal's work as "British hip-hop", a hopelessly lazy tag bequeathed on to him by less-informed journalists. Not only does this fail to shed any light on what this album sounds like, it also does no justice to grime music as a unique genre of musical expression, suggesting that it is indistinct from American rap. In truth, British rap and grime are completely separate from one another... Do NOT approach this as a rap album, or you will be perplexed to no end.' As Dizzee has always said, 'I don't have a label for it, it's just music, innit?'

Overall Dizzee wanted to maintain his old mantra 'keep moving'. Whether it was a success or not, Dizzee wanted to make sure that *Showtime* showed progression from *Boy in da Corner*, telling the *Guardian* soon after the second album's release, 'I think I tried to go a bit deeper [than in *Boy in da Corner*], technically as far as verses and stuff like that. I wanted to show deeper skills. The first one was a lot more hook orientated and simple, but I wanted to make something different for the second. There was a lot of speculation as to whether I could do it again, the curse of the Mercury prize and all sorts.'

Within the music industry *Showtime* had cemented Dizzee's place as someone who was here for the long haul rather than a mere fad, although there was still a feeling that he had more to prove, and Dizzee knew it...

13

SUPERSTAR

Dizzee's second album had put to bed any feelings in the industry that he was a one-hit wonder, but Dizzee knew that he had to continue making headway in the singles charts if he was going to win over the mainstream music-buying public. And the only way to do this was to continue releasing singles.

To sell singles in the mass-market manner that Dizzee and his label desired, he had to complete the transformation from underground star to pop star, and in order to do this a musician must complete a whirlwind of promotional appearances. The trick is to maintain credibility through the standard and quality of the music. On the promo circuit of 'Stand Up Tall', Dizzee must have begun to question the hoops the media required him to jump through just to sell a few records.

On a promo appearance on MTV's *Total Request Live*, he was famously asked, 'Now, we want to see how fast you can rap. You're up against Britney Spears and Rolf Harris. You've got fifteen seconds...' At the time Dizzee was still relatively new to the mainstream and wasn't quite sure if this was the kind of stunt that would best promote his image. He looked at the TV producer, and during a brief pause he gave the woman a look that said he did not want to trivialise and humiliate himself by having an MC battle with a video of Rolf Harris, not even for the sake of massive exposure on MTV. It looked like Dizzee was calculating the lack of street cred versus the bump in record sales in his head at that very moment.

On the other hand, Dizzee has never made a secret of his desire to be a mainstream popstar, and has always felt that the more people who like your music the better, even if that does seem like 'selling out' to bitter purists. So after a brief, reflective pause, he happily said, 'Cool,' before taking his seat in the green room to spit out a mind-boggling eighty-six words in fifteen seconds. Britney and Rolf never really had a hope.

To promote his new record, Dizzee threw himself into the TV and radio media circuit with ever-enthusiastic gusto, refusing to moan or whinge about the hectic schedule involved. During this time he rubbed shoulders with teen pop stars, reality TV stars, boy band members and anyone else in search of the limelight, all in the name of self-promotion. Outside, hordes of autograph-hunting kids were waiting for Dizzee, and it was at about this point that he realised he'd become a different kind of famous. He'd become a popstar. And the fact that his music wasn't quite 'pop' didn't matter.

In November 2004 Dizzee released his second single from *Showtime*, 'Dream', which became another top 20 hit for the young star. It sampled (and used the chorus of) Captain

Sensible's song 'Happy Talk', which was originally from the musical *South Pacific* by Rodgers and Hammerstein. The 'Dream' music video consisted of a mock 1950s-style children's marionette show depicting scenes corresponding to the lyrics about Dizzee's youth: street culture, crime, teenage single mothers, pirate radio and garage clubs. At first Dizzee wasn't sure about working with all the puppets, telling Elisabeth Donnelly of *PopMatters*, 'I dreaded it. It was weird – a little bit with acting and all that. It was weird because there was nothing to act with, there were just the puppets and all that. It was good, though, it was a learning experience.' The single was also released with a live performance of 'Imagine' as a B side, as well as two unheard tunes, 'Is This Real' and 'Trapped'.

'Dream' continues with Dizzee's biographical style, but rather than the bitter adolescent from the first album, this track shows a more reflective side with his lyrics.

The mash-up of the childlike verse and rap is a bizarre mix of musical genres and was one another sign of Dizzee's fearless attitude towards experimentation. It's a trait he's well known for these days, which has and always will set him apart from most other urban acts. Dizzee was also demonstrating his ability to take himself lightly and poke fun at himself and his music. It was widely haled by the critics as 'a track that you will either love or hate', but whatever the reception by the public, it is undeniable that lyrically, 'Dream' shows a more mature, less angry artist than the teenager in *Boy in da Corner*. It's a track that shows Dizzee's unpredictable nature and, even if it isn't to your taste, you wouldn't forget it in a hurry. Overall, the new happy, cheeky Dizzee people saw through 'Dream' intrigued them.

As Uma Uthayashanker said in *MusicOMH*, 'Although

this song may take a while to grow on you, Dizzee Rascal is undoubtedly a fresh and talented representative of British music and no matter what material he throws at us, his style is definitely something that will prove to be successful time and time again.'

'Dream' became Dizzee's longest-running chart-positioned song, with eight weeks in the top 75. It was his fifth top-40 single, and his second consecutive hit in the top 20, eventually peaking at number 14, his second highest position.

Dizzee went into the Christmas period of 2004 riding high. His music was enjoying chart success and his career was on a steady upward trajectory. He was even becoming a bit of a national celebrity. So much so that he was invited to contribute to the celebrity charity event of the decade.

The biggest stars in British pop music all squeezed into a London studio in November 2004 to record the twentieth anniversary version of 'Do They Know It's Christmas'. Twenty years after the greatest rock stars of the eighties collaborated on one of the most famous songs of all time, the icons of the noughties got together to record their version, and Dizzee was one of them.

The track was recorded in one day and included a diverse band of artists – Chris Martin from Coldplay, Dido, Robbie Williams, Ms Dynamite, Will Young, Thom Yorke, Busted, Keane and Snow Patrol – all of whom gathered in a converted church in north London under the guidance of original organisers Bob Geldof and Midge Ure, who were responsible for a seminal moment in pop history in the eighties, which raised millions for famine relief.

The first Band Aid single raised £8 million in aid for Africa and kick-started Live Aid, the global pop concert that raised more than £60 million for charity. When they recorded the original version it was, by all accounts, 'mayhem and chaos'. Stars drove themselves to the studio; Boy George was famously woken up in New York and told to catch Concorde in order to arrive in time.

This time around it was a more polished affair, with heavy media attendance and the ever-watchful gaze of the paparazzi. Many of the stars, including Geldof, arrived at the recording with their children and Blur's Damon Albarn served everyone tea and biscuits. Unlike the first time, all the performers knew what influence the single would have. As Geldof told the *Guardian*, there's 'a cultural and political resonance there wasn't twenty years ago.'

Many of the new generation of stars told the *Guardian* about their childhood memories of Band Aid. 'I was eight years old when the first one was out and it was probably my first memory,' said Gary Lightbody, lead singer of Snow Patrol. While Grant Nicholas from Feeder talked about how he'd bought the record and attended the Live Aid concert at Wembley.

Alongside Dizzee, the queen of urban music at the time, Ms Dynamite, was there, and she described the new track as sounding 'very now'. Another hot young black talent of the moment, Jamelia, apparently almost cried when she met Bob Geldof. The atmosphere was 'absolutely fantastic', she said. 'It sounds corny but there is a lot of love in the air.'

Dizzee made history again when he became the first artist to add lyrics to the iconic song since its initial recording. On the spot he came up with the lyrics that summed up the sentiment entirely, impressing everyone around him.

Apparently Dizzee wrote and recorded his part in just fifteen minutes, which isn't a big deal according to Dizzee, who told *LeftLion* magazine, 'I went there and they told me what they wanted. So when I wrote it, it was nothing. I did a recording of it, and I got shown afterwards that it was too short. So I just went upstairs quickly and wrote the rest of it, then came down. It's no big story really, it was just a good thing to do.'

Everyone was impressed with the young star, according to Fran Healy from Travis, who said Dizzee 'wrote a rap on the spot and nailed it'. It was a truly special occasion, where the combination of different stars created a unique vibe. 'Magic moments have happened,' said Midge Ure at the time of Dizzee's contribution. 'Justin [Hawkins] from the Darkness was standing there watching Dizzee Rascal do his rap bit in the middle and we were thinking, "Wow, that was fantastic." All the boundaries that musicians put up between them – I'm a rock star, you're a rap star – have disappeared.'

For Dizzee it was a very quick experience, but he was happy to be involved with such illustrious names: 'To be honest I wasn't there that long. I went upstairs, they told me, "two bars," I wrote it, said it, recorded it. Did another two bars, did some interviews for twenty minutes and then left. It was always gonna be like that… Maybe it's because everyone else sings. Mine was the first ever rap. I did meet the lead singer of Travis. Ms Dynamite was there. Sugababes were walking in as I left. Midge Ure, I met him. It was cool, man, but everything was all pleasant.'

It was extremely noticeable twenty years ago that there was a real lack of black artists in the line-up, but this time around, with Dizzee's presence, as well as Beverley Knight, Shaznay

Lewis, Lemar and Skye from Morcheeba, there was a distinctly black feel to the song. When asked about such doors being closed to people from his background, Dizzee replied, 'Yeah, man, that's why you have to kick it down!'

The single became the UK's biggest seller of 2004 as well as the Christmas number one – it was the first time Dizzee had made it to the top of the charts but it wouldn't be the last. The charity single was first played simultaneously on The Chris Moyles Show (on BBC Radio 1) and the breakfast shows on Virgin and Capital Radio, at 8a.m. on 16 November 2004. The video was then broadcast in the UK simultaneously over multiple channels, including the five UK terrestrial channels, at 5.55p.m. on 18 November 2004, with an introduction by Madonna.

There was an issue when people had problems downloading the track from Apple's iTunes Music Store. A partial solution was reached after a few days, though, enabling UK users to download the song at the standard iTunes price, with Apple donating an extra amount to the Band Aid Trust. British artist Damien Hirst designed an intimidating cover for the Band Aid 20 single, featuring the grim reaper and a starving African child. However, this was later dropped after fears that it might scare children. The single was released on 29 November 2004, with all money raised going towards famine relief in the Darfur region of Sudan.

The single sold 72,000 copies in the first twenty-four hours after its release and went straight into the UK charts at number 1 on 5 December 2004. The CD version sold over 200,000 copies in the first week, and became the fastest-selling single of the year. It stayed at the top for Christmas and the week after, holding on to the top spot for four weeks, just one week shorter than the original had done in 1984.

The whole experience meant a great deal to Dizzee, who told *DMC Update*, 'Well it was my first number one, so obviously a big moment. Chris Martin, Bono, Joss Stone and the rest of the group all around me, surreal. But to be honest, I was in and out of the studio quick time. The single sold 200,000 copies in the first week and became the fastest-selling single of the year.'

2004 had passed without any major negative incidents for Dizzee, and closed with him at the top of the charts and his second album selling well. Things were looking good for a big 2005. He was in for a minor dip in March of that year when he released the Double A-side single 'Off 2 Work'/'Graftin'. It was the third and final single from the *Showtime* album, although 'Off 2 Work' was a new track that didn't appear on either of his albums. The accompanying music video featured Dizzee in various ordinary workplace situations – as a policeman, fast-food vendor, businessman, etc. – and as Prime Minister, announcing his engagement to Cherie Blair, but it proved to be Dizzee's lowest-charting single to date, peaking outside the top 40 at number 44. The track was very dark, when compared to his more up-tempo releases at that time, and many of the critics liked it for its bleak reminder of the social ills and the competitive streak that was – and still – rife in the streets, homes and offices of the capital.

The track, dedicated solely to the streets of London, sends out a message that London is not 'all teacups', said Alvin Ross Carpio in *Socialist Review*. 'He also uncovers the realities of his ends with the complementary music video where council flats, estates, and alleyways are shown during a murky night in the streets of east London. There is a clear contrast between the high-rise council flats and the towering buildings of Canary Wharf also shown in the video.'

There was a feeling that this was some of Dizzee's darkest, grimiest work and perhaps that was why the public didn't go for it. Steve Hands of *MusicOMH* claimed that 'Tunes like "Graftin'" may be as ill-lit and foreboding as the arches that stretch over London's Eastend, but nowhere does the aural graffiti sound ugly, artless or overcooked.'

If Dizzee felt deflated, he needn't have been. It was the third and final release from his second album, and while it wasn't a major hit he was still seen in a positive light by people in the music industry and he was still selling records.

Outside the music business he was beginning to be seen as something of a street style icon, too. His hat n' hood look was being copied around the UK and soon the commercial labels wanted a piece of Dizzee's image. In 2004, he signed an international endorsement deal with American clothing label Eckó, as part of their move to recruit up-and-coming European artists. He shot the clothing campaign in New York in the spring of 2004 for their autumn/winter collection that year.

Dizzee was pleased to bits with the recognition he was getting from the wider hip-hop fraternity, telling *AllHipHop*, 'England we are coming up. Sometimes though, people emulate what's coming from the United States. There aren't that many people in London doing anything original. There was a time where people were dressing up with the champagne and all that bullshit, but niggas like me had hats, hoods, making our own beats doing our own shit and making our own way.'

Dizzee's always been into fashion and as he's earned more

money he's spent more on clothes, not that he'd ever need a stylist, he told the *Independent*: 'I've always spent a lot on clothes. In my underground days, because I'd make quite a bit of money… I like to look good, but not to the extent that I need a stylist.' Dizzee's always been too grounded for 'bling' and outrageous diamonds, though, and when asked by the *Independent* if he thought 'diamonds are a rapper's best friend'? He replied, 'Diamonds are not on my agenda right now. I'd put buying a house over buying a diamond any day.'

In 2005 Dizzee was such a big name that Nike invited him to design a trainer. Of course it came with his Dirtee Stank trademark of a steaming mound of poo surrounded by buzzing flies in the shoe's tongue as well!

Dizzee had been a major fan of the brand since he was a kid. His relationship with Nike continued in 2009 when he released another special edition trainer, the Nike Air Max 90. Made in partnership with Dizzee, Nike Design and Dizzee's long-time collaborator and creative director Ben Drury, who also designed the album cover for *Maths + English* and *Tongue n' Cheek*. Dizzee described his Nike Air Max 90 as 'Stylish but simple. The Air Max 90 is pretty much *the* street shoe, innit? It's quite sporty, but when you get the right colours you can wear it with anything. But with this one we tried to keep it quite plain so it could complete any outfit. It's functional and there was a pretty deep design process involved.'

Dizzee likes to make sure his trainers fit with any style and are sporty but casual. As he told *GQ*, 'The kind of trainers I like complete an outfit. It's my favourite shape. It's not too bulky. It's still a running shoe, but it doesn't look too much like a running shoe.' The trainers sold out in minutes, with trainer junkies even now bidding insane prices on the internet for the limited-edition trainer. All the proceeds went to the Summer University programme in Tower Hamlets, which Dizzee is now a patron of. Most people approved of the style of the trainer, according to *GQ*: 'The shoe is surprisingly thoughtful in execution also, with off-white leather and suede, although it lives up to its name with a pink tongue ("Most people's tongues are pink, innit?") and the logo of Dizzee's Dirtee Stank record label on the sole.'

Dizzee is famed for his love of trainers and has been known to wear a pair only once before chucking them or giving them away – he's not alone in this as apparently David Beckham does the same – but things have changed since then, claimed Dizzee in an interview with the *Daily Mail* in 2007, where he said he'd grown up and become less wasteful. 'For about a minute I got into the "wear things once and throw them away" mentality,' he says. 'But I realised it was just keeping up with the Joneses so I stopped.'

Dizzee's look has become iconic now and while it is has developed over the years, there are a few key items that are unmistakably Dizzee. He's famed for his baggy hoodies, loose-fitting jeans and stylish trainers, and he's pretty loyal to a few labels: 'I've always worn hoodies but they're fashionable hoodies. I like the urban look. I love jackets from Maharishi and my jeans have to be baggy. My favourites are classic Levi's 501 in dark denim or something from Evisu, all topped off by a pair of Nikes from my huge collection.'

He's also known for his belt buckles, which often have something funny written on them. He picks them up when he's shopping in the States and feels they're a big part of his personal style and identity: 'A belt buckle can make a powerful statement. I like to buy them when I'm in Los Angeles or New York so no one here has anything similar. I wear them with big black leather belts. You can change your whole look with a belt buckle. My current favourite says, 'Love thy neighbour'. I really like the mixed message – a huge bruiser of a belt buckle with a homely touch. It makes me laugh.'

Even Dizzee admits that he's made some fashion howlers over the years, though, the most famous being when he wore odd trainers to an interview at the start of his career. 'Wearing one black trainer and one white trainer was a big style error. Unfortunately, it was a look I tried out on a day I was being interviewed. There was lots of talk about whether it was some sort of statement but it wasn't that deep, honestly.' It looks like Dizzee set a trend, though, because years after he pioneered the look, in the summer of 2010 the hipsters of East London jumped on the bandwagon and wearing odd trainers became the look of that summer. Once again, it would seem that Dizzee was ahead of his time.

Unlike most US rappers, Dizzee's never been a massive fan of bling. While he wears a few pieces, he's relatively understated and keeps it to a few simple items. 'Big bling jewellery may look fine in the US but it doesn't work over here. I always wear gold, never platinum, and I wear the same things all the time: a Cuban link chain, which was a gift to myself when I got a record deal, a gold-and-diamond bracelet and two rings.'

As for tattoos, Dizzee revealed in the *Daily Mail* interview that he also tries to keep things simple, with just the one tattoo at the moment, of an eagle's head, although he is thinking of getting more.

'My only tattoo is on my right arm. It's an eagle's head with the words, 'Fix Up, Look Sharp' above it, the title of a single from the album *Boy in da Corner*. I'm thinking of one across my shoulders saying, '"Warrior".'

Dizzee's has admitted that one of the biggest problems he has when trying to look good is keeping his skin clean and spot-free. 'I break out in spots when I'm stressed. Skin care is a real problem for me. I've tried lots of different washes and soaps but they just don't work, at least not for me. Nowadays, I just use cocoa butter on my body but on my face I've been told the best thing is just hot water.'

Dizzee will always retain a sense of his original style unique no matter how big he makes it. Even at the GQ Awards in 2009, when all the guys turned up looking like James Bond in various Savile Row suits and tuxedos, Dizzee turned up wearing a fitted red D&G puffa jacket. 'I was going to wear one [a suit], but then it came last-minute and I'd just come from Ibiza the same day and I didn't want to wear a suit that I'd already worn,' Dizzee told *GQ*'s Jamie Millar. 'So I went looking round – I think I went round Selfridges – and picked up some shit that just felt right at the time... What I fucking paid for this jacket, I want to make sure I keep wearing it! I've got a few suits. I don't wear suits a lot, but I look good when I do.' When he's trying to be smart, Dizzee considers some of the Italian designers to be the best. 'A Gucci suit is still my number one,' he says.

Meanwhile his love of trainers hasn't altered and when asked in an interview by *GQ* magazine if it was true that he had sixty pairs stashed away, he replied, 'Probably more. I've got boxes at home from when I moved house. So I've probably got a few more.'

14

UNDER PRESSURE

In March 2005, just before Dizzee released his third single from *Showtime*, 'Graftin'', he was pulled over by the police. The BBC reported that Dizzee was a passenger in a car stopped by police in East London on Wednesday 2 March 2005, and that Dizzee was arrested together with the thirty-four-year-old driver. According to the police, 'They were both taken into custody at an East London police station and they were later released on bail to return on April 8. The driver, a 34-year-old man, was subsequently arrested for being in possession of a section-five firearm – pepper spray – and an offensive weapon, which was an ASP baton, and cannabis. A 20-year-old male passenger [Dizzee] was also arrested for being in possession of pepper spray.' Three other men in the car were searched and released. Dizzee was really upset with himself and thought he'd let himself down. 'That was some stupidness,' he later told

Dummy magazine. 'Didn't even get to court. I got caught with some pepper spray. Stupidness. It could have been worse. I could have really been in trouble.'

At the time it could have been a major roadblock in Dizzee's career. The initial issue was that he was due to perform in Salt Lake City, Utah, on 8 April, the day he had been told to report to a London police station to answer bail. He was then hoping to go on a major US tour for the rest of April, taking in major cities such as Los Angeles, San Francisco and Chicago, and a criminal record would have had a big impact on his visa for the States, who might not allow him into the country.

Thankfully for Dizzee the charges were dropped and the US tour went ahead. This time around Dizzee would be touring as a more established artist with a genuine fanbase in the States. One of his most successful gigs was in Doug Fir Lounge in Portland, Oregon, which Gray Gannaway reviewed in *In Music We Trust*: 'I expected Firs to be only sparsely filled with slightly curious coolkids (especially taking into account the fact that Dizzee's show came the night after DJ Premier of Gang Starr headlined a free 5-hour Scion DJ event at Holocene), but what I found was a packed club of avid fans, most of which could sing Rascal's songs word for word, an amazing feat in itself given Dizzee's thick British accent and rapid-fire flow.'

Dizzee performed with his partner Scope and DJ Wonder. He started off the gig with 'Sittin' Here', the first track from his debut album, wowing the crowd by bursting into a hectic a capella. He then went on to perform tracks from both of his albums, with the main highlights including 'Jezebel', 'I Luv U' and the crowd-friendly encore 'Fix Up, Look Sharp'.

Dizzee's shows went down a storm with the US media and Gray Gannaway went on to report that, 'As great as Dizzee's albums are, his live show is even more mesmerizing and comes across as a bit more rap-oriented. Good sonic representation is key since his thick, synth-filled and distorted drum production is the most captivating element of his sound.'

Much to Dizzee's dismay he was described as a 'fugitive from justice' in the Houston Press because of his recent arrest. Dizzee has always tried to disassociate himself from crime and violence. He's too wise for that and knows the kind of trouble it's brought some of his peers, such as 50 Cent and So Solid Crew. 'It's not the music that's violent,' Dizzee told online magazine *The Situation* at the time. 'When something's that close to the streets, in the inner-city, people go to clubs and sometimes they don't get along and sometimes people end up getting hurt. That's the negative side. With time, as it grows, it will get better.'

On this US tour, Dizzee paid a visit to Canada where British urban music has more of a following. Back in the nineties drum and bass artists like Aphrodite, Andy C and Mickey Finn made a big impact there, so Dizzee's label, XL, felt the market was ready for the next best sound to come from the streets of London. In Toronto, Dizzee played to a mainly white middle-class hip-hop and drum-and-bass-loving crowd of almost 850 people.

He performed with his old Roll Deep buddy, DJ Wonder, who hyped up the crowd with a thirty-minute set of grime's greatest hits to date. Wonder dropped tracks from Kano, D Double E, Lady Sovereign and More Fire Crew – the idea being to boost the genre as a whole and get the novice crowd up-to-date with the sound of Dizzee and his contemporaries.

As the lights dulled, Dizzee and his hype man bounced onto the stage to do their tour intro 'Sittin' Here', the opening song on *Boy in da Corner*.

As Dizzee launched into the a cappella segment of his show, which had become a hallmark now in this part of the world, Matthew McKinnon of *CBC* noted that, 'His accent makes him hard to follow at the best of times. Here, in a gloomy room with underwhelming acoustics, his voice sounds like a buzz saw.' Dizzee then went into a full hour set of the best tracks from his first two albums: 'Learn', 'I come direct when I inject and I'm expecting your respect'.

The audience, quite baffled by Dizzee's accent, sang along aimlessly: 'The crowd sings along when it can, though the effort feels like placing a bucket under a waterfall,' said McKinnon.

Club-goers tried to get into Dizzee as much as they could but the cultural divide was highlighted when DJ Wonder got the best reaction from the crowd when he mixed in familiar US beats from hip-hop hits such as 50 Cent's 'Wanksta', Dead Prez's 'Hip-Hop' and The Notorious B.I.G.'s 'Juicy'. It would seem Dizzee still had a way to go before winning over the foreign crowd. As McKinnon reported, 'Some minutes later, waiting for transit outside the show, one concert-goer turns to another, "Did you like that?" "What?" "DID YOU LIKE THAT?" "Oh. Yeah! But probably more if I understood a single fucking word."'

It would appear that in North America Dizzee still had his doubters. People claimed that America would never 'get' grime or Dizzee Rascal, but Dizzee would never accept that kind of negativity: 'Grime is growing outside the UK with me,' he claimed when he returned from his US tour. 'I'm the pioneer of grime! Whether it will grow production-wise depends on the individual and how far they will take it without restricting themselves. With grime, where it's really coming from the streets, kids are growing up now and recognising it as their own. They are pushing it forward, and I think it will grow into something big.'

On Dizzee's US tour in 2005 he went to the southern states for the first time, to the home of crunk, which Dizzee has always claimed was one of his and grime's major influences. 'The closest think to my thing was crunk,' Dizzee said of his main influences in his early grime days. On his trip to the 'Dirty South' Dizzee hooked up with some of crunk's main players, such as Bun B, Matt Sonzala and the Grit Boys, and made some strong connections with what he feels are grime's closest relatives. 'He's [Bun B] like an uncle or something, he just looks after man. He's really humble, down with it – serious dude. I was introduced to him the first time I was out in Texas by Matt Sonzala. We went on *Damage Control* and did a set with the Grit Boys... Matt's really safe. He's with it, very professional. Most people down south are cool, really laid back.'

Dizzee was wowed by the famous 'southern hospitality' and felt that the isolated nature crunk as a genre had a lot in common with UK hip-hop: 'With them [southern rappers] they've had to do it for themselves for so long that they've got that really independent mind frame. That whole southern hospitality thing is real, they're quite warm.'

But Dizzee also got a lot of respect in other regions, especially on the East Coast, where Dizzee got to perform with hip-hop superstar Nas: 'I've got to show love for the East Coast. Nas, he put me on stage with him when he was at the

Forum. It was wicked, an experience to be onstage with him. I done that with Pharrell but Nas, that's a rap god.'

One of the big differences between the UK and US scene is how the labels are run, as many of the guys who head up the urban music labels earned their stripes on the scene first. In the UK the labels tend to be run more by traditional businessmen who don't always 'get' the music and want to dilute a lot of the hard-edged artists they sign. People like Lyor Cohen and Jay-Z are the label big wigs in the States, and they've been a part of the hip-hop scene for almost as long as it's been around. Nick Cage highlighted this difference between the UK and US urban music industries in *Resolution* magazine in 2005: 'We met Lyor a couple of months ago in Puerto Rico at a confer- ence with all these American hip-hop DJs and I realised that, at heart, he's just a big music fan. That's how he got into it, and now he's taken it to the max. We don't have people like that in the industry here in the UK. Most of the people at labels don't understand, they're just chasing a buzz, they ring up their six key people and get the same name back, but they don't really know how to take it forward from there. In America you've got two or three development entities between the artist and the label.'

Enlightened by the US way of doing things, Dizzee decided to reignite his old label, Dirtee Stank, with an ethos 'about bridging the gap between indie, majors and the street.' Like The Streets' Mike Skinner's own company, the label would still be affiliated to XL – as would Dizzee, who had one more album to go on his three-album deal – but Dizzee and the artists would have full creative control. Nick Cage was also in charge at the new label, whose aim was to give more talented kids like Dizzee a chance: 'It's what I'm trying to do on a ground level, work with kids who have some talent and try to develop it further, but I'm doing it all on my own.'

Dizzee wanted to invest some of the money he'd generated from his two hugely successful albums, *Boy in da Corner* and *Showtime,* into Dirtee Stank. The idea being to offer an alternative to the way the major labels tended to misrepresent urban artists. 'Majors don't fully understand the scene,' said Dizzee at the time. 'They try and water it down and it doesn't work. That's why I'm working on Dirtee Stank. Dizzee felt that the music industry had been one of the great let-downs in his life and that by having his own label he could help make a change. When asked by the *Guardian,* 'What has been your biggest disappointment?' Dizzee didn't miss a beat in replying: 'The music industry, for not being the magic carpet ride that you think it is before you get into it.'

Dizzee felt strongly that many labels were approaching the urban music industry with wrong attitude and signing the wrong artists. 'As ever, the majors are jumping on the wrong things and consequently stemming the possibilities for other artists,' explained Cage. 'There's a massive gap between what you would call an underground label and a major record label. We're trying to find a way to bridge that gap.'

According to Cage, Dirtee Stank exists to promote gifted artists with 'social problems' that other labels might be scared of. 'People who, through the conditions they live in, might not be stable. The label should also help artists overcome hurdles such as access to studios that "take something from a raw demo to something people will get excited about on the street".'

Dirtee Stank's first signing, Klass A, fitted the bill perfectly.

The rap trio from Leicester were initially signed to XL, where they'd supported Dizzee on his *Showtime* tour, but they'd struggled to make any headway with the label. As Nick Cage recalls, they were good but need some street-level hype, which they'd been missing: 'A label on its own cannot make an artist hot. They can market it and cross it over to the general media, they can put it in boxes and sell it for you, but they can't make you hot, not in this kind of game. With the sort of music I work on, the heat has to be self-generated or be done at this level down here.'

Dizzee was a big fan of Klass A from the off and felt he had to be involved with them as soon as he heard them. He told *LeftLion*, 'They actually signed to XL before I did. I don't know what their situation was, but I heard their music and I was feeling it. It touched me and around that time I just had this feeling, like this hunger. So from there I just knew that something has to come from outside London and then one day it was just there. It was always there, but I had to grab hold of it and bring it through Dirtee Stank.'

For Dizzee, signing an act was a huge progression in his career. 'Signing a band is a major step for me, I'm really happy,' he said at the time. 'I feel like I've found the best next thing to come out of England. They're coming out around the end of this year.'

Although Klass A never found any great success, Nick Cage claims Dirtee Stank set a new precedent when they allowed the artists to exercise full creative control.

The other major signing at Dirtee Stank was Newham Generals, who signed as Dizzee's flagship act in 2006. Listeners of Rinse FM will know their regular show. The East London

grime collective formed after the joint decision of D Double
E, Footsie and Monkstar to leave N.A.S.T.Y. Crew. The crew's
name comes from one of D Double's lyrics: 'If you mess with
the Newham General, you'll get left in Newham General.'
Under Dizzee's guidance, they have released a mixtape and an
album – *The Best of Newham Generals* and *Generally Speaking*
respectively – though the latter wasn't seen as a grime release
due to the distorted lyrics and strange beats. On 7 December
2009, the Generals released the single 'Hard', which is a
crossover song. It was well received and got a lot of airplay
on Logan Sama's show during October and November of that
year. However, these days, the act is made up of just D Double
E and Footsie, since Monkstar found God. 'His MySpace
caption says, "Doing it all for Jesus,"' Footsie told the *Observer*.

Dizzee finds working with the Newham Generals like going
back to his early days, and he likens them to early rave act The
Prodigy. 'They're like a black Prodigy,' Dizzee told *Giant Step*.
'The last couple things they've done is some amazing shit. For
me it's like *Boy in da Corner* all over again... the sound, the
intensity and the quality of the music...'

Newham Generals are known for their energetic live shows
and up-tempo style, and for believing in bringing grime back
to its rave roots. 'A lot of people forget that grime is supposed
to be dance music,' Footsie says. 'If you go to its nearest relatives, they're hard house and techno, but that's got lost a bit.
What we've done is put it back, but keeping a lot of grease in
the lyrics. We're not smooth-faced kids saying some mindless
stuff that's really shocking to mums at home.'

Dizzee used to listen to D Double E on pirate radio when
he was a drum and bass DJ years ago, and he used to knock

about with D Double E's brother in Bow: 'I've always admired D Double. I grew up with his brother, some of his family are from Bow. I hung around, grew up, did all sorts with his brother so I knew him already. We did radio a lot, 'cos I used to be on with N.A.S.T.Y. Crew and that. I always had him in mind – I listened to him as a kid. He was one of the people who inspired me to MC.'

Now Dizzee was guiding one of his youth idols, who he felt could have a universally appealing sound that went beyond the boundaries of grime: 'Newham Generals are a group from the London pirate radio scene,' Dizzee told *The Student Pocket Guide*. 'You've got Footsie who MCs and produces a lot of the music alongside Cage. D Double E is middling a bit in production but he's a very well-known MC in the underground scene and has been for a few years. I originally knew him from listening to drum and bass on Rinse FM. We signed them. They've got their new album coming out so we've just been putting the last bit and bobs together over the past couple of months and they'll be ready to fly out at the end of this year. They're shooting their first video in a couple of weeks. I personally compare their sound to a black version of The Prodigy. People know them as grime or whatever but I think the sound is as big and as universal as The Prodigy. Obviously a bit edgier 'cos they're coming from a street angle.'

Whenever Dizzee gets a chance he tries to give Newham Generals a plug. He introduced his act to *NME* as 'a group from the London pirate radio scene. The grime scene, whatever you wanna call it – it's all interlinked. One of them is called D Double E the other is called Footsie. Footsie produces music and he's also an MC. D Double E's an MC, he does a bit of production as well, actually. I met them through the same scene, pirate radio. And I'm putting their music out on my label Dirtee Stank.'

The Newham Generals spent a few years supporting Dizzee's shows before releasing their debut album in April 2009. The album was well received by the critics, getting three stars from Paul MacInnes at the *Guardian*, who liked the old-skool vibe: 'The abiding sound is one of revivified rave, revisiting British dance music of the mid-90s in the same way US producers such as Bangladesh and Kanye West have been approaching hip-hop of the same period. The single, "Heads Get Mangled", matches filtered vocals to a creepy fairground scale. "Supadupe" is a dark, heavy anthem that at long last makes the link between east London and the Dirty South.'

The third and most recent act to sign for Dirtee Stank was Smurfie Syco. Widely predicted to be 'the next Tinie Tempah', Smurfie is billed as being Dizzee's new prodigy. He got his name because he was small and always had an attitude, he tells *Grime Forum*: 'In my family I've got loads of brothers and sisters and we all had nicknames for each other. My one was Smurfie 'cos I was really short. In my area, when I used to run about with my friends, they called my Syco, 'cos I was this little terrier. Then, when my friends started to come over to my house, they would hear my family call me Smurfie and get confused. So in the end they called me Syco Smurfie. When I signed up to Myspace I switched it around and it stuck from there.'

Smurfie signed for Dizzee and Nick Cage because he sees them as heroes with a good eye for artist development looking towards the future: 'It's kinda like Justice League, ha ha! Or maybe Ninja Turtles – Cage would be Splinter with the guidance and knowledge! I've been eager to do things and got excited about situations only for Cage to say three or four things and change my mind completely. He sees things way in advance, and is great at making the decisions – which you can see in Dizzee. All the decisions Dizzee has made, Cage has been instrumental. Justice League is a good name for them because they are superheroes to me. Even though we're friends, it hasn't clicked for me yet. I'll hop off the tour bus with Dizzee and see people react crazy...'

As ever with Smurfie the Dirtee Stank ethos holds true, where Cage ensures the artists have absolute control of their craft, unlike at the major labels, where they try and mould them into something they think will sell. 'He [Cage] won't crush my artistry. Seriously, when my album comes out you will see stuff everywhere! He allows me to do whatever I want and then he'll give me the guidance. It's up to me to accept it. Karate kid can never tell Mr Miyagi how it's gonna go. He has to listen and interpret it. That's what I'm doing. I'm not scared to take risks.'

Smurfie got Dizzee's attention by continually pestering him through social networking sites like Myspace: 'I kept on trying to contact Dizzee through Myspace and sent him links to my music all the time until one day he replied and that was where it all started. He was on tour in a different country when he replied to me and since then I was signed to his label, and although Dizzee doesn't really A&R me, due to being overly busy, the Dirtee Stank team look after me on that side of things.'

When Smurfie first signed with Dirtee Stank, he told

Dizzee to keep it a secret so he could get on with making music without any hype or attention: 'When I first signed I told Dizzee, "Don't tell anybody I've signed," and for six months, nobody knew. Everybody there thought I was an office clerk or something; sorting stuff out on the phone, helping the tour manager. I wanted to figure out what I was going to do first. It eventually got round that I was signed and so I got recording. I made my first single "Where's Your Head At?", and after performing it live it got such a good reception that Dizzee wanted to come onto the tune. So for me that's a sign I'm doing the right thing.'

Like Dizzee, Smurfie's sound is a mad mix of various influences, which he feels is reminiscent of his mentor's earliest work: 'It's a crazy mix. I ain't given it a label just yet but it deserves one though 'cos it's really good! It's melodic and quite old fashioned. I never really owned any music in my house so I listened to a lot of music that at first I hated. I didn't jump out of my mum's womb and straight into reggae! Now, though, when I hear those sweet melodies on a Sunday morning when my grandma's cooking or something I can just vibe. There is a mad mix in my music – I can hear it all in there. On this mix CD I listened to it top to bottom and it is grime. It's not quite what is going on today, but it reminds me of those *Boy in da Corner* days. I know that's a big thing to say, but on one track that Dizzee features on ['Clappin''], it could have made it onto *Boy in da Corner*. If not *Showtime*. It's definitely that era of music. It's a conscious tune too – it's not reckless.'

For the most part, hype is being built around the star through small gigs and YouTube uploads. In April 2010, Paul Lester of the *Guardian* – who also predicted the rise of Tinie

Tempah – hailed Smurfie as a big star for the future, reviewing his tracks in a very positive light, saying that, '"Don't Start Nuffin"' is heavy, pounding grimestep (a genre we think we just made up), all deep, growly, reverberating subsonic bass, distorted drums, and computer-game bloops and bleeps. "I'll Be Back" samples Arnold Schwarzenegger in *The Terminator* and is heavier than The Prodigy doing Led Zep's "Trampled Underfoot" produced by Kode9. "Crush" is dancier, "Where's Your Head At?" samples Basement Jaxx, while "Hellrazor" is powerful dub-grime. Grub? Dime? He really is all over YouTube like a rash.'

For Dizzee, going back to running his label felt like the grafting days of his early career. 'Before I got a record deal, before I was on pirate radio or anything, I used to make tapes and have MCs come around for the fun of it,' he told CBC. '[Running Dirtee Stank] feels like going back to that. I like the idea of finding good music and showing it to the world.'

Being both from the street and part of the mainstream, Dizzee feels he's in the perfect position to help artists who were once like him make the transformation from pirate radio to MTV: 'We add a pinch of both worlds. I have an understanding as to what it's like to be in the mainstream; not at the Snoop Dogg level, but enough to understand the ins and outs of it. And, obviously, I'm from the street. I did the whole underground thing and was one of the pioneers when it comes to the grime thing. We were the first to be selling thousands of white labels. I can definitely bridge the gap and make big things happen, man.'

Touring with his signings is a good way for Dizzee to give them exposure, but he also likes the way he can reflect on his career by bringing through new talent: 'For me it's refreshing touring with Newhams and Klass A because you get to kinda see yourself again, from a next perspective. Because obviously I couldn't see how I was then 'cos I was right in the centre of it. The whole bigger picture you get to see... understand why people feel, how they feel.'

Dizzee loves the idea of trawling the underground for the freshest talent. It's a good way for him to keep his finger on the pulse of what's happening with the street-level music while his pop career escalates. 'I've had the label from before I was signed to XL,' he explained to *LeftLion*. 'I was putting out tracks like 'I Luv U' and a couple of instrumentals, which were around on pirate radio and the underground scene. Now, finally, I've been lucky enough to come across some groups that make good music and bring them along. Dirtee Stank is about showcasing and giving people across the country the chance to hear it. I'm a fan of music so it's another side of me. It's a blessing.' But some people feel that Dizzee has brought some artists up without allowing them to come through the ranks in the traditional way, an accusation to which Smurfie harshly responds, 'I would say to them that Dizzee wouldn't be where he is today if he couldn't make good decisions. If you respect him and think he's a smart guy then respect his decision to sign me and wait and see.'

15

FLEX

Towards the end of 2005, British hip-hop and urban music began garnering a huge following for the first time. A new crop of British urban music artists were getting rave reviews, snapping up major awards and achieving chart success along the way. There was a feeling that a sea change in British urban music was underway and that Dizzee was leading the charge.

It wasn't just Dizzee out there on his own, though, the British scene was full of successful artists. In September 2005 the MOBO Awards picked UK artist Sway as the world's best hip-hop artist, overlooking US heavyweights such as 50 Cent. At the time Sway was an unsigned, largely unknown British rapper, and winning the award was a definite sign that the UK's street stars were ready to challenge American domination of the scene.

2005 saw Lethal Bizzle, Kano and Dizzee's old crew Roll Deep gain chart success. *Touch* magazine ran a special on the meteoric rise of British hip-hop, with Sway, Lethal Bizzle, Klashnekoff and Killa Kela on its cover, backed by a Union Jack.

'It was partly because we wanted to reflect the fact that there are a lot of strong artists who are all doing something interesting,' said *Touch*'s deputy editor Chris Blenkarn. 'What's happening now is very exciting and there is definitely some potential. But there have been false dawns before and no British artists will make it to the top until TV and radio stations get behind them and fans dig deep. I'm always sceptical about it. I hope it does go further, but until people start putting bums on seats then it's hard to say.'

The major issue at the time seemed to be that radio and TV stations were still playing considerably more US than British urban music. Lethal Bizzle, who originally made his name on the grime scene with More Fire Crew and scored a number 11 solo hit with 'Pow' that year, agrees and told the BBC at the time that they needed to back UK acts more: 'We don't have Radio 1 playlisting our records, or all these other outlets supporting us to the fullest potential. Once that happens, this whole music game will really take off. It's just a shame that right now there's only few outlets that are really supporting it.'

Sway, however, felt that it wasn't anything to do with support and that it had more to do with the fact that UK urban music isn't good enough. 'Artists just have to be professional and realise that if they've got a product that's worthy of being exploited, there are going to be people who are going to want to exploit it for financial gain. A lot of people in the UK are bitter saying, "They don't want to support us." Just get your game up.'

When Dizzee's old friend Wiley was asked by the BBC about the British urban music revolution, he wasn't as optimistic as everyone else on the scene, despite recently getting to number 11 with Roll Deep's 'The Avenue'. 'In England, it's a new sound and everybody's not as open-minded as you think. However, that picture is changing as we begin to recognise and embrace even more our local heroes and realise that alongside the Americans the par is level. I think the quality is out there. But as with anything new and fresh and sounding original, it takes time for it to penetrate, to get under people's skins and for them to have a serious long-term reaction to that in terms of buying records.'

Dizzee's old friend DJ Semtex was also pretty negative about British urban music's prospects: 'Obviously we're never going to be as good as the Americans,' he told the BBC. 'When it comes to the UK market, what are you going to buy – Eminem or the UK Eminem? You want the proper Eminem.' Semtex felt that the best tactic for UK artists was to maintain their British nature and forget about trying to be American. 'We're in this totally different league to the Americans – we've got a totally different society, we've got a totally different way of thinking. That's what we've got to take into consideration. We're British, not American.'

Going into late 2005, the big question on everyone's lips was whether or not grime could be the vehicle – with Dizzee behind the wheel – to get British urban music played all around the world. The media was full of chatter about how the interest generated in America by Dizzee Rascal had cast a spotlight on other acts in the grime scene. The summer of 2005 saw Lady Sovereign sign to major US label Def Jam Records, and that August saw Wiley and his Roll Deep crew try and break the US with a few New York dates. Dizzee's old crew were keen to ride the wave of success they'd garnered in the UK with a cross-Atlantic push. Their album at the time, *In at the Deep End*, was doing well in the UK, but Wiley wanted more: 'We made our album for the whole country,' Wiley told the *Telegraph* in October 2005. 'And now we want to take the music international.'

Roll Deep had moved away from the darker grime vibe Wiley had come to symbolise in favour of a more pop-based hip-hop sound. Unfortunately for Wiley and the other four members of Roll Deep who accompanied him to New York, their performances attracted less interest than they must have hoped for.

The *Telegraph* reviewed the show at the time saying, 'In truth, "East London's finest" seem out of place, chatting lyrics in their UK patois over syncopated electronic clicks and whirrs that sound alien compared to contemporary US rap.'

Wiley was still determined to make it in the US, telling the *Daily Telegraph* he was jealous of US hip-hop stature and prominence. 'I like their independence. No one tells them what to do.' He even talked about how he'd like to leave Britain and live in New York. 'I like it up in Harlem. I think I might move there. When I'm here I can't help thinking about all the pioneers of rap and how they couldn't have imagined that their music would turn into a huge industry. Maybe in ten years' time, people will look at what we're doing now in the same way.'

But they didn't seem to hold Dizzee's new-found popularity against him though – they were moving in different directions in any case – despite their many reported differences at the time. In August 2006, Roll Deep made an appearance on MTV's *TRL* and denied that there was any beef between them and Dizzee. 'There's nothing with him personally,' they said. 'He chose to do his own thing and he's opened a lot of doors for us, so we can't hate what he's doing. I mean, there were obviously some discrepancies, but hey, he chose to go on his own.' When asked if they'd ever accept Dizzee back into the crew, or collaborate with him, they appeared open-minded: 'We'd like to, but we don't know.'

Other artists trying to bring the grime scene into the mainstream and across to America were Kano and Lady Sovereign, both of whom began making serious headway in 2006. Kano came up through the underground scene along a similar route to Dizzee. He was a year ahead of Dizzee at Langdon Park School and the two of them used to know each other in their early teens from the East London's pirate radio scene. Like Dizzee's best mate back in Bow, Danny Shittu, Kano was a promising footballer who had played for Chelsea, West Ham United and Norwich City by the age of thirteen. In the end, though, he abandoned his sporting ambitions in favour of a musical career.

Kano first came onto the music scene with N.A.S.T.Y Crew, of which D Double E used to be a member and from which Dizzee's Roll Deep originated: 'I've actually known Kano since I was about fourteen or fifteen,' recalls Dizzee. 'From pirate radio, though we kinda lost touch, I was floating about, I didn't even know he was MCing so when he came into N.A.S.T.Y Crew I was like, "Rah, he's back again."'

Back in the day, Kano's N.A.S.T.Y Crew was one of the most popular acts on pirate radio station Deja Vu on Monday nights from 8 to 10p.m. Through the crew's popularity, Kano launched his solo career, breaking out with the track 'Boys Love Girls', which was produced in 2002 and later remastered by Dizzee Rascal. Kano's debut solo album *Home Sweet Home* was released in 2004, along with his debut solo single, 'P's & Q's', and he battled Wiley on *Lord of the Mic 1* in one of the most famous grime clashes, despite being only seventeen – the result was seen by most as a draw. Kano has since had four top 50 albums and spread his musical wings beyond the underground scene, collaborating with the likes of Craig David, Blur's Damon Albarn, Kate Nash and Vybz Kartel. Like Dizzee, Kano's been heavily criticised by grime traditionalists for abandoning the genre in favour of mainstream recognition, but that's never bothered him. He continually retorts that he's an MC who can rap over all music, telling the *Independent*, 'I've been doing the MCing thing at raves and on the radio and people criticise me by saying I'm an MC, I'm not an artist. I want to show I can make songs. I've worked with producers who have challenged me to write something more detailed, less straightforward.'

Lady Sovereign – also known as Sov – was another artist making moves into the mainstream at the time and was being hailed as the 'Queen of Grime'. Like Dizzee, she grew up in some of London's roughest estates. Sov's Chalkhill estate in Wembley has since been demolished because of its dilapidated state. Lady Sovereign started her career by rapping over beats on the Internet and Jay-Z famously signed her after asking her to freestyle for him, Usher and L.A. Reid on the spot. She's the only non-American female ever to be signed to Def Jam Records and has supported Dizzee on a few gigs. Alongside each other they were responsible for pushing urban music boundaries around the world.

Dizzee was still the champion of the UK scene at home and abroad, and in 2006 he cemented his rise to the top with more exposure than ever. Dizzee's first appearance in a feature film saw him play a cameo role in *Rollin' with the Nines*, and he also contributed a track to the soundtrack. Dizzee described the film as being 'like the first black British gangster film. It's like *Snatch* or *Lock Stock* or something, but on a bit more of a serious tip.'

Dizzee's evolution into acting had always been on the cards. Like other great black urban artists before him, such as Will Smith, Ice Cube and Snoop Dog, it was inevitable that casting agents would coming knocking. It was only a small role where he played a crack dealer, and he does more teeth-sucking than talking, but it was Dizzee's first chance to put into practice the skills he'd learned as a kid at drama school.

Dizzee spent most of 2006 doing live shows as he began to get offers to appear at all sorts of mainstream events. The summer of 2006 was booked up with festivals such as the Reading and Leeds festivals and he was also set to tour with huge American rock band the Red Hot Chili Peppers. However, Dizzee's oddest appearance of 2006 saw him speaking at the Oxford Union on 10 May 2006. Some of the great minds of the past two centuries have spoken at the 189-year-old university, including Ronald Reagan, Richard Nixon, Yasser Arafat, Pervez Musharraf (and Kermit the Frog), and Dizzee was set to join this illustrious list. The video of a group of intellectual Oxford students dancing awkwardly to 'Fix Up, Look Sharp' became an instant YouTube hit. Dizzee was honoured to be asked to speak at Oxford, especially as he'd never had much of hope of getting in as a student, and he told the *Daily Mirror*, 'It felt good because I'd never have been asked to go to Oxford any other way. It was good to be there on my own terms. People wanted to see me for who I was and what I did.'

This wasn't his first visit to Oxford, though, as Dizzee had made an earlier appearance at a black-tie ball there, playing 'Fix Up, Look Sharp' to an audience dressed in ball gowns and dinner suits. In another example of his ground-breaking nature, Dizzee claimed it was one of his career highlights to date, telling the *Observer*, 'It'd make people think twice about Oxford University, I can tell you. That is one of my major achievements – coming from Bow... Thanks!' But he didn't have any plans to make it a regular event. When asked if he planned on making an annual appearance, he responded, 'That'd just be greedy. There's no point in chasing that first high – it's never the same.'

Between his live shows, Dizzee spent a lot of time working on his third album, which he told the *Guardian* was going very well: 'Now I'm in the middle of the third [album]. I've done a lot of it and if I do say myself it's banging. Quote me on that please... It's called Maths + English because that's what I do. Producing is all numbers, it's Maths and English, obviously, the writing, and where I'm from England. It says it all, man. I've done a few tracks on it with D Double E and Footsie, for some production that's on more that grimey take. I've also done a thing with Shy FX, so I'm branching out, man, all over the place, but there definitely is a vibe about it.'

By mid 2006 Dizzee had been around the world – the

States, Argentina, Chile, Brazil – and of all the places he'd visited, the latter touched a real chord with Dizzee because of the poverty and harsh conditions faced by many of the country's youth: 'Brazil was interesting. The show was massive but it was quite hard at the beginning. Seeing the poverty just shows you how fortunate you are here. I didn't need to get to the favelas, just seeing kids scuttling about... real poverty, in a place so beautiful – the contrast is very ugly. Poor kids... it's deep. It's not nice.' Dizzee was also inspired by the music he'd encountered in this part of the world, and he felt that there were great symmetries between the style of the London ghetto and that of Brazil's favelas: 'I love to hear music in its own environment. That is something I will take away from me for ever, that's priceless. I heard that baile funk – it's Miami bass with Brazilians chatting over it. It would be grime, if it were here. I could get with that. But the older traditional stuff, like the bossa nova, that's what I was feeling. I bought a couple of CDs, coching in my hotel or on the beach. That's good music, definitely.'

Dizzee's live shows had created a big following and he worked hard while he was on tour to make sure he put on the best show possible. He claims that being on tour is hard work and that he has to remain focused to give the audience the best possible experience: 'I take it very seriously. My eye's always on the ball. The fun part is being on stage. That's when you can let loose. Everything else you have to keep your eye on. If you don't treat it like work, like it's not a business, you slip up. I'm a music lover but I'm in the music business. It's two different things almost.' Even at the after-show parties, Dizzee would never have much of an opportunity to unwind as he'd be meeting music execs. At times it would feel like he was working non-stop, even in his time off: 'You might go out to a club and that can be like work itself because you end up networking. It don't really stop but at the same time do you want it to? It'll stop if you want it. Then you'll be that person who used to be famous who everyone still recognises but you're broke. Ha ha ha fuck all that though, that's long.'

Dizzee's live show had transformed since his early days of playing raves like Sidewinder with Wiley. He'd grown in terms of stature, stage presence and confidence. New and different forms of music had been incorporated into his show, allowing him to play to a more diverse audience. Because of his far-reaching style he was able to tour with the likes of the Red Hot Chili Peppers and The Prodigy. The latter, he says, are one of the best live performers he's ever seen: 'like going to the biggest baddest rave ever!' Dizzee looked and learned from these greats and incorporated some of their act into his own show, particularly the rock elements that inspire moshing at his raves, something not usually done at rap gigs. 'My shows are pandemonium!' Dizzee says. 'People go crazy at my shows like it's a rock concert. They mosh and do mad shit. I'm a boy from Bow in East London and people mosh like it's Megadeth.'

When Dizzee's on tour there's usually a fair amount of time spent partying but it isn't always out in the clubs as you might imagine. he likes to play consoles in his trailer: 'I love going on tour, working up the crowds. During the day in America we were always on the computer playing Xbox. Sometimes after the show I might have a spliff to calm down. Or just be alone, sit down and breathe. I go from extreme to extreme – there ain't no in between.'

16

NUMBERS & WORDS

In Dizzee's brief moments away from the tour bus in 2006, he spent much of his time writing and preparing his next album *Maths + English*. In an interview with the grime blog *Blackdown* at the start of 2006, he talked about how he'd started jotting some stuff down in preparation for the new album, which he'd already decided to name *Maths + English*: 'I put a couple of music ideas down. I haven't really completed anything as such but I've got a couple of things there still. Not a full album yet but I will be getting on it. It's *Maths + English* because it's straight game. That sounds very American, but handling your business, that's *Maths + English*. It's what I do as well as far as lyrics, writing, money whatever. Whatever you do, it will be one or the other – if not both.'

As ever, Dizzee was keen to expand his musical horizons. He wanted to create an album that pushed him more into the mainstream with its mass-market appeal, while maintaining the high standards he'd set himself: 'I'm just trying to do things that I haven't done before, again. Trying to widen, reach the masses a bit more. Try and make the best music I can.' At the time Dizzee had established a sound ethos for making good-quality music that sold on a large scale. With his next album, Dizzee was keen to elevate himself into the realms of the great musicians of our time, such as Marvin Gaye and Snoop Dogg, artists who transcend genres: 'I think if you mean it, people will pick up on it. Sincerity. You might not be into soul but you know who Marvin Gaye is, or if you're not into hip hop but you know who Snoop is – they've reached people because they mean it and they've established themselves. I'm on that.'

By early 2007, anticipation for the new album was at fever pitch amongst Dizzee's fans and within his close circle. But it would appear that some people couldn't be trusted. Before the album's official release in June 2007, there were reports of tracks being leaked on the internet, much to Dizzee's annoyance. 'He's fuming,' Dizzee's publicist told Scott Wright of *Clash* magazine. 'I wouldn't like to be around if he finds out who did it.'

While he was angry about the leak, such occurrences, and the media hype that surrounds them, were all signs of the widespread interest that Dizzee was attracting through his music.

By 2007 grime had bubbled back down to the underground after the initial flurry of interest that surrounded it following Dizzee's Mercury Prize had died down. With Dizzee's change of style over the years came a barrage of criticism from the underground, who claimed that he'd forgotten his grime roots and sold out. But Dizzee has always claimed that it's unrealistic to expect him to stay the same and not evolve: 'Sometimes you get people talking about "he ain't grime no more", but they don't understand. Grime was just me making the most of the little that I had. What do you want me to do? Give up my record deal? It's not 2001 anymore. I've grown up. Physically. Mentally. So there's no point in me trying to sound like I did five years ago.'

Maths + English was two and a half years in the making and had proved to be the biggest challenge of Dizzee's career. Up until then he'd been known for his speedy work in the studio – it took Dizzee no time to make *Boy in da Corner,* and with his second album he was so eager to capitalise on his success that he produced it in a matter of weeks. With the third album Dizzee was obsessed with getting everything perfect, so he took his time: 'Both of them other albums, I knocked them out. With *Boy in da Corner,* songs took a couple of hours, but on this one there's songs that I worked on for weeks.'

Dizzee also revealed in an interview with *Giant Step* that it wasn't so much perfectionism that made his third album so time-consuming, but the hectic schedules of everyone involved. Dizzee was considerably busier than he had been when he'd started out, but he still enjoyed making the album, despite the lengthy process. 'It was a lot more fun than anything I've worked on before. Songs took months, literally,' Dizzee recalled. 'Big tracks like "Sirens" and even "Da Feelin'". "Da Feelin'" probably took the longest because I started working on what I at first had thought would be a single. We got Joss Stone on it... just loads of different things on it. Just back and forth, back and forth for ages because [producer] Shy FX was out of the country, then I was out of the country, just shit like that.

Dizzee was conscious of the fact that he didn't have the wealth of inspiration and motivation around him that helped produce the first two albums, so he took his time over the third to ensure its perfection. 'First album – you've got a lifetime to work on it. Second album – you try to make a different album to the first one, but you want to keep moving quickly. This one I just wanted to slow things down and really think about it, come with it properly and make it perfect.'

There were rumours that success and a long break between albums meant Dizzee had lost his way, but nothing could have been further from the truth. With its big-budget production and genre-transcending nature, *Maths + English* was set to be the album that launched Dizzee to even great heights.

There was a strong feeling that Dizzee was moving completely away from his grime roots, but he was unapologetic about this new direction, claiming the grime scene had a lot to thank him for: 'There wouldn't be no grime without me. I'm humble, but I don't feel that I have to make a grime song every time. Grime is recognised around the world now, it's a beautiful thing, but so is drum and bass and so is rock. Can't I make some of them songs as well?'

The first single from *Maths + English*, 'Sirens', was released on 21 May 2007. Dizzee needed an explosive track to mark his comeback, and 'Sirens' most emphatically fitted the bill. The song bursts open with such explosiveness that it comes as a shock to the first-time listener. On the track Dizzee's character and flow are as tight as ever, but there's a more solid song structure than we've heard before. Dizzee blurts out three incredibly tense, action-packed verses, which get louder and more unhinged as the track progresses, and a crackling police radio stutters over the deep booming bass. Dizzee's love of rock is the foundation behind the track – 'A part of it was inspired by Korn's "Here To Stay".' Dizzee later told *HipHopDX* – where a blaze of tapped cymbals and gnarly rock guitar climaxes with a massive rebellious breakdown.

The song opens with a banging drum intro (performed by Dizzee) and the Korn track that inspired it had been a favourite of Dizzee's for years: 'At my shows we used to drop a big Korn tune called "Here To Stay". That tune is so heavy. I play drums on "Sirens" and that's where we got our ideas from. I'm a proper fan. I even went to see them last time they were at the Forum.'

Whilst the style and production is progressive, Dizzee has gone back to his roots on this track, which gives another bolt of insight into the tough streets of East London. Its hardcore nature makes it a record you experience as opposed to enjoy. *NME* summed it up perfectly when they hailed 'Sirens' as 'a record that sounds like a crime scene, one that surveys the tattered newspaper hoardings – stabbings in East London, hoodied youth gone feral – and thrives off them. Not a pleasant record. But a great one.'

Lyrically, Dizzee has gone back to his 'I Luv U' style, using a strong narrative to tell a gritty street story – 'that old-school storytelling shit' – of Dizzee getting arrested for assaulting someone in a mugging. It talks of how he was 'snitched' on and the tragedy of being sent to prison. But, as ever, he shows his thoughtful side when he comments on the shock he feels at the severity of the assault.

But Dizzee is unrepentant by the end of the song, showing

the brutal attitudes of kids on the street. Dizzee has made no secret of the fact that this story is autobiographical, and his participation in the real-life incident that inspired it was not as the victim. He told the *Observer*: 'It's not clever, it's not good.' He shakes his head shamefacedly. 'I'm definitely not proud of some of the stuff I did as a youth, but that's where my mind-frame was at one point in my life, and I can't pretend those things didn't happen. I'm not glorifying them, I'm trying to make them into art...'

Dizzee goes on to explain in his interview with Ben Thompson that he's surprised by how easily people have taken to the track and that to some it's nothing more than urban voyeurism: 'The whole song is just wrong really... There's been lots of positive responses, but no one's actually said anything about the content... I guess. Everyone likes a little urban story.'

The video isn't as hardcore as the song. Instead it takes on a different tack by showing Dizzee as the victim – he's symbol-ised as a fox in an urban fox hunt. The video is packed full of blatant symbolism about Britain's prevalent class and race divide and the negative connotations these entail. Despite it looking like an East End estate, the video was actually shot in Romania – another foreign experience for Dizzee, where he encountered a raw untamed urban culture not unlike his own. 'They've got estates over there that look just like ours,' Dizzee explained to the *Observer*. 'Except there are still bullet holes in the buildings... and that's in the nice part. It's definitely being opened up a bit, because they've just joined the EU, but away from the touristy areas it's a deep and eerie vibe. It's like my friend over there was saying, "The facade is thin" – it feels like anything could happen at any time, and sometimes, it does.'

The critics loved 'Sirens'. It was hailed as 'the most exciting rap record of the year' by *MusicOMH* who went on to claim that 'the Rascal has come of age'. The single was playlisted on BBC Radio 1's 1 Upfront list and the music video made the top 30 of that chart.

Despite disappointing levels of airplay on television and radio, the single was a chart success, returning him to the top 20 in the UK Singles Chart after his last release – 'Off 2 Work'/'Graftin'' – was the first to miss the top 40. The song peaked at number 20 and became his fourth top-20 hit. It was also his first single to be released on 7-inch vinyl.

'Sirens' might have harked back to some of Dizzee's earlier work with its edgy, close-to-the-bone nature, but the rest of the new album, *Maths + English,* was Dizzee's most progressive and unfamiliar work to date. To help morph his new sound, Dizzee collaborated with a wide range of stars: the Newham Generals; grime star Jammer; UK pop princess Lily Allen; Southern US hip-hop act UGK; Joss Stone (though she was later edited out); Arctic Monkeys' Alex Turner and Shy FX, who was brought in to collaborate on a track and produce the entire album.

Having grown up listening to drum and bass as a kid, it was DJs like Shy FX who'd inspired Dizzee to get into music in the first place. The two had plenty in common. Like Dizzee, Shy FX was a pioneer – of jungle, London's black urban dance music of his time – and he brought the underground genre into the mainstream with hits such as 'Shake Your Body' and 'Don't Wanna Know'. And just as Dizzee had tried to convert the US to grime in the mid-noughties, Shy FX had tried to take jungle to the US in the mid-nineties, where – rather comically – he'd had to try and teach them how to dance to it. He recalled in *Clash Music*, 'I remember going to New York in 1994 with the SOUR label and putting jungle in front of two thousand ravers who'd never heard it before, and didn't know how to dance to it. What did we do? We jumped into the crowd and started shocking out, showing them what to do...'

Having come up through the underground scene and been elevated to chart success, Dizzee and Shy FX had a lot in common – it would be the start of a professional partnership that would last until his latest album, *Tongue n' Cheek*.

Everything about Dizzee's new record was a leap forward from the past. Take the bright pink sleeve, that was a clear statement that he was trying to break through to the bubble-gum pop audiences. The album opens with 'World Outside', which serenely whooshes out a dazed dreamy ambiance, with edgy knife-sharpening percussive clinks, a subwoofer-stressing bass and a chorus. The album's intro track is supremely apt as the rest of the album shows exactly what he means by this 'world outside of the ghetto'. Both lyrically and musically Dizzee takes the listener on a journey of his life since leaving the estates of Bow, taking in a few celebrity friends – Alex Turner and Lily Allen – new US acquaintances – UGK – old brothers – Wiley – and new mentors – Shy FX.

To call the album 'grime' would be incorrect, while its roots could be in nothing else. Save for the track, 'You Can't Tell Me Nuffin'', there are few signs of actual grime on any part of the album. Dizzee would just label it as 'music' but this album sounds more like UK hip-hop than any of his others. Meanwhile some people were hailing the album as Dizzee's long-awaited foray into pop – or maybe eclectic pop. Whatever it's labelled as, the album is very catchy and danceable. In hindsight it seems like a natural progression from his biggest hits up until that point, 'Fix Up, Look Sharp' and 'Stand Up Tall'. And it's in those tracks that you'll see the early foundations for *Maths + English*. Throughout the album Dizzee displays his epic versatility as he mixes and mashes genres with no regard for purity or tradition.

There were a few murmurs of disapproval when it was heard that Lily Allen would be performing on 'Wanna Be', as some felt it had the potential for disaster. But her fun-filled cover of Bugsy Malone's 'You Wanna Be A Boxer', is a welcome lighthearted addition to the album.

Dizzee felt that, musically, himself and Lily blended together easily and they both got on well, even if Lily didn't return Dizzee's calls for while. He told the *Mirror*, 'With Lily Allen, we just clicked right away. It was easy, no pressure.'

Dizzee shows his Southern crunk style in 'Hardback (Industry)' – the punchy rhythm over sinister synth strings wouldn't sound out of place on a Lil Jon or T-Pain album. On 'Where's Da G's', Dizzee manages to blend his own sound into crunk by employing a Southern bounce during Bun B and Pimp C's verses. Dizzee was proud to have enlisted two of crunk's legends, telling *Clash Music*, 'We're close, man. They've showed me a lot of love. I'm proud of that track. It's real, uncompromising. Two of the fucking legendary gangsta rappers on a grime beat.'

Lyrically, the song pokes fun at the fake gangsters and egos involved in the urban music scene. Dizzee wanted to try and poke fun at the nonsense some rappers spout about themselves, trying to make them look tough and hard: 'That song was really just supposed to be a cocky thing, just being a bit cheeky, like, "Let's dick around and make a song about fake G's,"' Dizzee said. 'A lot of these songs just start out with lyrics and eventually I find the beat that goes with it well and there's a marriage between them. It was a conscious thing as well, like people taking this whole "G" thing a bit too serious and most people ain't really been through enough to really justify it. Not that I'm someone who's crying about it but... I'm just kind of pointing it out.' Dizzee clearly feels the whole association between crime and black people is getting ridiculous and does nothing but harm: 'Soon you'll have to be a fuckin' mass murderer before you can be a rapper. It's getting a bit ridiculous. And where is it getting black people?'

Dizzee displays a personal take on fame in 'Paranoid', when he raps about people trying to exploit him because of his success. He even goes into a kidnap plot on the track. Dizzee went into the truth behind the track in a subsequent interview with the *Observer*, where he spoke about how certain friends had changed their attitude towards him since his success: 'They were meant to be my friends as well. When you start to make a bit of money, people switch on you. They get the wrong end of the stick. They think you're this or that, but really it's just that they miss you. And 'cos of the kind of people they are, they don't deal with it properly: they can only respond with violence. But then, when they actually see you, they realise, "Oh, he ain't changed that much really"... They weren't really gonna kidnap me, they were just yapping.'

Dizzee leaps back to his grime roots with the punchy, knife-stabbing beats of 'You Can't Tell Me Nuffin'', which seems to be a dig by the people left behind in the estates and on the underground scene who were dissing him at the time for leaving the streets and not being true to his roots – they knew the truth and he didn't need to prove it to them.

Dizzee again rolls back the years when he shows that there's still a place for garage in the post-grime world with 'Flex', which was a hyped return to the two-step sound that Dizzee first MC'd in his early pirate radio days with Roll Deep. He expands his versatility even further when he collaborates with Shy FX on the drum and bass number 'Da Feelin'', an up-tempo, happy track that shows an all-new side to Dizzee. He then cements his intentions for the album to be a summer soundtrack with 'Bubbles'. With its head-bobbing, funky buzzing bassline, the track demonstrates his production skills and ability to create and MC over any type of music he likes.

His versatility is again underlined in 'Temptation', where he samples a chorus from the Arctic Monkeys' B side, 'Temptation Greets You Like Your Naughty Friend'. It was recorded alongside tracks that appear on the Arctic's second album *Favourite Worst Nightmare*. Talking about the collaboration in *NME*, Dizzee recalled the experience of working with the hottest indie band in the country: 'We recorded it a couple of months ago in London. They sent me the track first and I wrote a verse for it. They came to London and I rapped the verse over what they had. We did it really quickly – in about half an hour.'

Dizzee told *Clash Music* how he then sampled the Arctic's B-side track in this meeting and went on to make 'Temptation', creating the first grime-indie track, or 'grindie' as Dizzee calls it: 'For the album I made a remix out of that track and put in a couple of extra verses. I didn't really think that much of it, then everyone I played it to started going crazy. I played it to Alex and them and they loved it. People are saying it's the first real grindie track.' Dizzee went on to explain how grime was breaking into the indie scene, even if there were a few cultural differences: 'Yeah, all the indie kids are into grime now. Bands like Hadouken! You can see they feel it.' He chuckles to himself.

Dizzee and Alex Turner became solid friends after working together. Dizzee was really impressed with Alex's skills and musical knowledge: 'I'd definitely like to work with them again, especially Alex. He's a special guy. He knows all types of music – it goes beyond rock 'n' roll.' Dizzee went on to tell *Clash Music* how impressed he was with how grounded the band are: 'You consider how big they are now, but he's still real. It ain't got to them, man.'

Dizzee and Alex began to hang out socially, even going to a karaoke night together for Alex's birthday with Alexa Chung and Kelly Osborne. Alex talked about that night on a BBC Radio 1 show, which Dizzee was guest hosting in place of usual presenter Zane Lowe. 'We went out for a bit of fun and games and Dizzee came along. We went out for a bit of karaoke, and I've never seen a crowd so moved.' Turner went on to reveal that they sang Warren G's 'Regulate' and Arctic Monkeys' 'I Bet You Look Good On The Dancefloor'. 'It were incredible, it went off! Dizzee stole the show, we might as well have gone off after that!'

But of all his collaborations, working with the now defunct UGK was perhaps the biggest deal. UGK (short for Underground Kingz) was an American hip-hop duo from Port Arthur, Texas. They was a stalwart of the crunk scene that's so adored by Dizzee and which he hailed as the closest relative to grime. Chad 'Pimp C' Butler formed the act in 1987 and he then joined with Bernard 'Bun B' Freeman, who became his long-time partner. Like Dizzee and grime their music was seen as a gritty outcast in comparison to the more shiny, digestible hip-hop.

Throughout the nineties UGK operated on the perimeters of the scene, without having much major commercial success, despite garnering lots of respect within the industry. But in 2000 they had a major breakthrough when they appeared on Jay-Z's monster hit 'Big Pimpin'', and they also appeared on Three 6 Mafia's hit 'Sippin' on Some Syrup'. Both of these collaborations greatly increased their profile round the world.

Like Dizzee, UGK had some problems with law, although their issues were more severe than Dizzee's. In 2002, Pimp C was imprisoned and as a result of his incarceration both members of UGK began solo careers. On 1 March 2005 Rap-A-Lot Records released Pimp C's solo debut, *Sweet James Jones Stories*. Bun B later released his own solo foray, *Trill O.G.*, on 18 October 2005, which reached number 6 in the US Billboard Charts.

On 30 December 2005, Pimp C was released on parole, and on 25 July 2006 he brought out his first post-incarceration album, entitled *Pimpalation*. It was at around this time Dizzee met up with the UGK and the pair were keen to work with the young UK rapper.

On 7 August 2007 the group released their fifth studio album, the self-titled *Underground Kingz*. The first track – 'Two Types of Bitches' – on the act's final album opened with Dizzee's collaborative effort. The album also featured a host of global stars including Talib Kweli, Too Short, Rick Ross,

Z-RO, Three 6 Mafia, Slim Thug and OutKast, as well as hip-hop legends Kool G Rap and Big Daddy Kane on a Marley Marl-produced track entitled 'Next Up'. The album went to number one in the US charts, selling over half a million copies, and it's now considered an all-time classic. Pimp C passed away in December 2007. Reportedly, the rapper died from a Promethazine/Codeine syrup overdose combined with sleep apnoea. His death was ruled an accident.

For Dizzee it was a big deal to collaborate with his crunk heroes, and especially poignant given the tragic events that followed. He spoke about the experience of working with UKG to *Giant Step*: 'That was one of the points where I felt like, "OK this is serious." Because I look up to them so much and I'm still a fan to this day and I still bump… good music. Pimp C's voice still empowers me, makes me feel like I'm the shit. I feel exclusive when I'm listening to that shit. I'm on their album as well. It's the first track on their album, it's their last album [together]. It's one of those mad things.'

It was obviously a shock for Dizzee to hear about Pimp C's death. Dizzee says they were quite similar to each other in temperament and Pimp C was always bigging up Dizzee: 'He told me, "You're a king, Dizzee." I'll never forget that. He was a lot like me in a lot of ways. He could be quite random and a bit loopy and quite excitable. I think that's where we connected. Now I know how I sound to people because I can get a bit like that.'

Dizzee and Bun B are still very close and speak regularly, with Dizzee always looking up to the man he considers family: 'Bun B, I kind of look at him as like an uncle or a big brother or something like that. We've got some similar traits. He can be pretty quick-tempered. But on the other side he really carries himself right, he's quite gentle and he's really well-mannered. He's a stand-up guy and quite worldly for a gangster rapper. He's probably one of the most intelligent people I've spoken to ever.'

With all the new sounds and collaborations, Dizzee was again taking a risk, but as a whole the critics were very impressed with Dizzee's new album. It was highly praised for its skill, diversity and progression, with the *Guardian* exclaiming that, '*Maths + English* is a reminder of just how talented an MC Dizzee Rascal is: the sound of his voice as it curls itself around tongue-twisting syllables is thoroughly satisfying.'

The *Observer* had even more praise and loved the genre-busting sensibilities of the new album, claiming it was his best work to date: 'Young Dylan Mills' third outing is his strongest, most ambitious and mature record to date. It's wider-reaching in its lyrical content – with Dizz declaring his intention from the opening whirl of "World Outside" – "There's gotta be more than this, man" – and, more importantly, in its musical range, from the radio-friendly, Bugsy Malone-sampling "Might As Well Quit", featuring playful gangster's moll Lily Allen, to the superbly radio-unfriendly "Pussy'ole". Essential.'

NME gave Dizzee's latest album a solid 7/10, stating that Dizzee had matured and redefined himself as an established artist in a less urban-orientated musical landscape: 'Stage One of Dizzee Rascal's career is complete, the MC is learning to live in Stage Two, where within the post-MIA, post-Lethal Bizzle, post-grindie Britain, he must find his place again. So far, just about so good.'

PopMatters was even more impressed, giving *Maths + English* a score of 8/10, hailing it as his best work yet: 'Rascal manages to outdo himself, releasing one of the most memorable and challenging hip-hop albums in recent memory.'

The only really negative comments come from Ian Cohen at *Stylus* magazine, who gave the album a C+ and called it 'flossy' and 'inconsistent'. Cohen felt that the wide-ranging nature of the album, with its multiple-collaborations, proved to lack any sense of completeness: 'The price of diversity is cohesion and there are points where *Maths + English* veers wildly off track, often the result of Dizzee flexing his fattened Rolodex.' Cohen goes on to highlight weaknesses in various tracks and concludes that these detractions override the album's attributes: 'Dizzee ends up with a record that will more likely be defined by its failures than remembered for the success it achieves more often.'

Thankfully the buying public disagreed with *Stylus* and concurred with the more positive media reviews. *Maths + English* entered the UK Albums Chart at number seven, one position higher than his second album, *Showtime*, which charted at number eight and much higher than the award-winning *Boy in da Corner*, which peaked at number 23. It ended up going gold in the UK having sold over 100,000 copies.

Maths + English was only given a digital US release initially as Dizzee began to take a less ambitious view towards cracking America. Dizzee had spent a lot of time in the States in the previous few years and he'd learned a lot about the cultural differences between the two countries. He now acknowledges that this is why it has been difficult for him to make it big over there: 'I've come to accept that it's a totally different place to where I'm from. Their mind-set and the way their environment works. Some people in America don't know there's hip-hop or even black people in the UK. I'm serious. I've met 'em.'

17

RASKIT DON'T GIVE A DAMN

The chart and critical success of *Maths + English*, coupled with his new collaborations and sounds, pushed Dizzee into uncharted genres. Indie was definitely the sound of the moment in the summer of 2007, with bands like Arctic Monkeys, White Stripes and Editors topping the charts. However, surprisingly to some, Dizzee was the object of much adulation from those on the indie scene. Dizzee decided to capitalise on this by playing gigs in the genre's heartland, Camden. Just three days after the release of his third album, Dizzee went out on to the North London streets to spread the word about *Maths + English*, playing an intimate gig at the indie-centric Proud Galleries. The venue was rammed full of chequered shirt and skinny jean-wearing white kids, who lapped up Dizzee's energetic show. On the night Dizzee enthused to *Time Out* about embracing his new fanbase, which had vastly changed over the years: 'I'm used to playing in front of indie crowds. My fans are lunatics. I encourage mosh pits, I encourage lunacy, I make music to let go to. When I started, I was making music for the 'hood but even back then I was still always into broadening out, into making music for everyone. I've accepted them as part of my fanbase. And besides,' he adds, 'they know how to mosh!'

The media was full of praise for Dizzee's ability to knock down the barriers between the heavily segregated UK music scene. But for Dizzee this was nothing new; he'd been consistently broadening his horizons ever since the 'Fix Up, Look Sharp' days in 2003, through to the Captain Sensible remix of 'Happy Talk' and right up to blending the Arctic Monkeys into 'Temptation' on his latest album. Dizzee had always demonstrated a willingness to stretch music to the limit and throw the musical conformists' rulebook out the window. 'I want to learn,' he told *Time Out*, 'and I learn more from different artists.'

At the time, despite the media frenzy, Dizzee was still very much alone when it came to creating cross-genre music. The majority of indie bands were still immersed in the same shallow pools of influence as previous generations. And within the grime scene, artists felt that it was more pertinent to stay within the confines of the genre. Grime still saw itself as raw and unpolluted, although the few who were breaking out were pushing ahead of the pack and making waves in other musical arenas.

Lethal Bizzle was one of the few to follow Dizzee's lead. Like Dizzee he had come up through pirate radio with early grime crew Mo Fire. In 2007 he would again take the same path as Dizzee by collaborating with a leading indie icon. In Bizzle's case he performed with Pete Doherty in 2007 at a gig at the Hackney Empire and he also played at London's punk HQ, the 100 Club. Both Dizzee and Lethal Bizzle featured heavily in that summer's pop and indie festivals, such as V, Reading and Wireless. The grime stars loved the unifying nature of their performances. 'It's about getting your music out there to people who haven't necessarily heard of you,' Lethal Bizzle explained at the time. 'I did Trafalgar Square's "Love Music Hate Racism" – it made me smile: black kids and white kids moshing together, singing together. It's good to see folk united through my music.'

Dizzee's never been happy about giving music labels, right since the days when the media coined the phrase, 'grime', for his debut album. But while Dizzee understands the need for various musical varieties to be given names, he doesn't think that should prevent musicians from transcending their genres. He's learned from some of the world's top musicians how to move between the various forms of music, and he thinks anyone who has an issue with that is just jealous: 'People classify things and that's fair enough. But if somebody wants to make something different, that doesn't make them any less of an artist. In each genre, I've been around the biggest. In pop I toured with Justin Timberlake, with reggae it was Sean Paul; I toured with Jay-Z and the Red Hot Chili Peppers. It's all an education for me, to see how they do it. People who criticise me are just jealous.'

It was at this time that Hamish MacBain and Simone Baird of *Time Out* made the very good point that grime had the potential to push beyond the boundaries urban music had created. In the past, they said, the limits that British sub-genres had created simply stifled their potential: 'In its rawest form, grime is as exciting a British music as you'll find, and to lose that character would be awful. But if it's to escape the cultish confines that hemmed in drum and bass and UK garage, then it must take on board other ideas.' The feeling in the media at the time was that through *Maths + English* Dizzee had become a beacon of light for the British music industry, showing the way forward for others to follow. There was a feeling that if British urban music were to make a global impact, other artists would have to follow in Dizzee's footsteps and reach out to wider forms of music. 'Dizzee's *Maths + English* shows the way forward. Besides Alex Turner, Lily Allen and Dizzee's drum and bass hero Shy FX are also on-board, helping the album ping-pong between club banger and chart stormer.'

For Dizzee, having an issue with musicians for branching out is just politics and has little to do with pure music. He hopes that eventually people will grow up and let artists evolve as they want to, regardless of their musical background. 'It might take a while, but that's why it's important to branch out. So hopefully the next generation, who might not have seen me come up through raves or whatever, will have less politics about their music.'

Dizzee's attitude towards mixing musical genres was not shared by everyone. Wiley felt that he was staying true to his roots and fans with his grime album *Playtime is Over*, which he shamelessly scheduled for release on the same day as Dizzee's *Maths + English*. In *Time Out* he indicated that his grime album was a way off staying loyal to his people: 'The fans said,

"Stay grime, everyone else changes." So I said. "OK, I'll stick as close to it as I can."'

Releasing the album on the same day as Dizzee's brought media attention to both the albums. Wiley was very open about his motives for releasing the album on the same day as *Maths + English*, telling the *Independent*, 'You have to do stuff like that. Because when someone goes into the shop, they're gonna buy both. I would. You can't see Dizzee and not think of me. You can't see me and not think of him.'

To understand Dizzee and Wiley's relationship you have to go back to their days on the estate. Like Dizzee, Wiley grew up in the mean streets of Bow, and before getting into music he led a life of crime and violence. 'When I was a kid, I was a shotter [drug dealer] and I sold stuff,' he recalled to the *Independent*. 'I've lived the life. I'm not a little boy, and if you want to say someone is coming from somewhere or he's come from the 'hood, or he's come from the ghetto, I've come from there still. So it's not all roses.'

Back in the early Roll Deep days, Wiley was Dizzee's mentor. He helped introduce Dizzee to the scene, getting him air time on pirate radio, slots at raves and generally garnering publicity within the underground. Wiley had a huge influence on Dizzee's debut album *Boy in da Corner*, even appearing on a track, '2 Far'.

Everything was great when they signed simultaneously for XL, under Nick Cage's management. However, things soon began to get complicated. Dizzee had a backlog of music to draw on and was able to produce his first two albums in a very short space of time. XL wedged Wiley's debut release, *Treddin' on Thin Ice*, between Dizzee's two wildly successful albums, *Boy in da Corner* and *Showtime*. The decision to flood the market with three underground grime releases made under very similar conditions by two people with similar backgrounds working very close to one another was always going to be difficult.

One single ('Wot Do U Call It', a song addressing the debate of the labelling of grime) made the top 40 in the UK charts, and the album sold roughly 20,000 copies, compared to worldwide sales of 250,000 copies of Dizzee's *Boy in da Corner*. On the up side, Wiley's album received decent critical acclaim and is seen as one of the foundations of grime's success as a genre. BBC 6 Music hailed it as 'the most original, and most English, album I've heard all year.' There were even a few voices in the States claiming that Wiley's work was an improvement on Dizzee's, with *Dusted* magazine saying, 'An album worth its bluster, *Treddin' on Thin Ice* finally delivers on the promise made by the two-step scene years ago. Along the way, it also manages to improve upon the snaky street rap of recent upstarts like Dizzee Rascal. Wiley's new release goes a long way toward legitimizing UK hip-hop as something more than just a passing trend.' Unfortunately for Wiley, the positive reviews didn't translate into tangible success. Feeling that he was playing second fiddle to XL's 'man of the moment', Dizzee, in the end he walked away from the label and Nick Cage's management.

He later explained the decision to the *Guardian*, saying that he felt the label was too heavily focused on Dizzee for it to work: 'I was in Dizzee's shadow. I was naturally jealous of him, and the label, XL, were focusing on him, and not really concerned about me.' Years later Wiley would reflect on their time at XL together in an interview with the *Independent*. He claimed the two musicians were locked in competition to be the best, which only strengthened the divide. 'I was an artist, he was an artist. I always used to want to be the best in the game,' he says. 'I always wanted to be the best at what I do but without treading on anyone. But you can't actually do it. But then so did he, Dizzee. So you start as friends… but then you work hard and you're practising what you've been doing, and it shows and it comes out until you become… not enemies, but competition. So it was natural jealousy that made me leave.'

On Dizzee's second album, *Showtime*, he responded in 'Hype Talk' by taking a poke at Wiley with his lyrics. Through a mock conversation questioning whether 'Wiley skipped da country left him?'

Meanwhile Wiley offered an olive branch to Dizzee by releasing the track 'Letter 2 Dizzee'. A nostalgic track in which he raps about their freindship when they were younger and ends by saying they're still brothers.

When he heard about this track, Dizzee insinuated to *Clash Music* that Wiley was overly preoccupied with him. 'I heard about that, he's obsessed. But it's not the same kind of song as my song, is it? Besides, I only gave him 8 bars at the end of a 16 in the second verse. He didn't even make it to the first verse.'

Dizzee later claimed he wanted to draw a line under the petty issue, which was just dragging him back into stupid behaviour. He wanted to get on with his music career, but admitted this was hard when Wiley kept going on about it. 'This whole situation', Dizzee told *Clash Music*, 'is just so very gay. But it seems to be a constant part of my life, 'cause he ain't gonna shut up. I would have done anything for Wiley, man, outside of music, and he knows that. That's why this has carried on for years. If I hadn't put this whole thing behind me, I would never have made *Maths + English*. We could be shouting things at each other for ever – that's what we did on the estate. It's normal, standard, just a habit – but it'd be a shame and a waste of music to fall back into that.'

Wiley spent most of 2006 in the studio, churning out grime hits through twelve underground mix CDs in eighteen months under his Eskiboy identity. The pressure to produce quality music nearly sent Wiley over the edge: 'I was going mad with it, and writing, every second,' he told the *Guardian*. 'I was just a studio rat for a while. I wouldn't leave.' He eventually sent a riposte to Dizzee on the mixtape *Tunnel Vision Volume 6*, which contained two tracks aimed at Dizzee. The first, entitled 'Reply To Dizzee', is a speech where Wiley tackles Dizzee's 'Pussy'ole' bar by bar.

Wiley then launched into an attack on Dizzee for refusing to play gigs that Wiley was playing: 'I step on stage and I come round the place, but he don't come round near me.' Wiley then goes on to attack Kano, Lethal Bizzle and Dizzee by claiming that they'd abandoned the underground scene.

The second track, '2nd Dub 4 Dizzee', is a much more aggressive response over a heavy, grime-infused beat: 'I couldn't be a pussy, I bin through too much… I'll let the hood decide, they can tell us who's better, It sure ain't the boy in the Dirtee Stank sweater!'

For Wiley the constant antagonism with Dizzee and the rest of the scene was wearing him down, and after the release of his 2007 album *Playtime is Over* and all the mixtapes, he made the bizarre decision to retire. Sure, his second studio album wasn't a commercial success, but he still had a large enough underground following to maintain a viable career. For Wiley it had all got too much and he craved a normal life, telling the *Guardian* at the time: 'I just want to be normal. I'm 28 and I'm tired. My last album will come out and all the mix CDs that I've done already, but that's it. I don't want to do it anymore... The grime scene doesn't even deserve me.'

In practice, though, Wiley's retirement was over quickly and within months he was back making music and doing shows, claiming that he'd just wanted to gain some objectivity: 'Now I've stepped out I can see better. I've calmed down. For the past seven years everyone's just been watching me, all the time I've been running around, fighting, getting stabbed... everything I've been going through they've just been watching me. So now I'm going to step out and watch them, and that might keep me going an extra 10 years.'

During this period, Wiley has seen the underground music scene evolve and start to establish itself, but he feels it will take a lot longer for it to fully form, and that he might even be too old to enjoy it by then: 'It takes 10, 15, 20 years to build a scene,' Wiley says. 'Which is another reason why I retired, because I thought, You know what, I'm 28 – when it's peaking I ain't even going to be here. I don't want to be Grandmaster Flash.'

Wiley feels that himself and Dizzee have opened up the mainstream for urban underground artists in the UK and is shocked at how young some of the new kids coming up are. No doubt he's thinking of people like Tinie Tempah and Smurfie Syco: 'now when I watch Channel U, there's a million kids on there doing their stuff... they're not even copying me or copying Dizzee, they're doing their thing. The kids... it's what they're saying, they're too fresh from school. Way too fresh.'

After his 'retirement', Wiley came back strong in 2008 with the release of an album *Grime Wave* and the track 'Stop Being Silly', again aimed at Dizzee, who he has a go at for being immature and driving a Mini – 'I've got a Bentley and you've got a Mini'. However, the track was largely overshadowed by the release of Wiley's single, 'Wearing My Rolex', which came out at about the same time as the album and became his biggest single to date, peaking at number two in the charts and becoming one of the summer anthems of 2008.

Finally Wiley had gained large-scale commercial success to match Dizzee's, although he claims he didn't turn his back on the underground scene afterwards 'When I done "Wearing My Rolex" I didn't turn around and say, "I'm gone,"' he told *Time Out*. 'I just went back to the 'hood and smiled and shared with everyone, you get me?'

Wiley has always been confident of his musical abilities and has consistently claimed that he's one of the best producers around. With his latest chart success he felt he had the momentum to outstrip the competition, including Dizzee: 'From here on, my music will show everyone. Because I actually am a good musician. I'm not just an MC. Tinchy or Dizzee can't chat to me 'cos they're not on my level when it's studio time.'

After gaining some perspective on their feud, Wiley has since become more placid and regularly reaches out to Dizzee. At awards shows he often gives a shout out to Dizzee and calls him out on Twitter. He initially suggested they do an album together, claiming they could 'do a million and not even have to see each other', before following up with a later tweet saying 'he doesn't want to die without him and Dizzee squashing their issues'.

Over the years Wiley has sporadically tried to make peace with Dizzee, and has often admitted to Dizzee's prowess as a musician. In 2008, in an interview with the rapper Bashy, which can be seen on YouTube, Wiley claimed that 'Dizzee is the best artist in this country today'. In the same year he told *AllHipHop* how *Boy in da Corner* (an album he still listens to) established grime, and how Dizzee taught him to keep it real in his music: 'Dizzee taught me one thing: "If you're not talking about something that you're going through, or where you're coming from, then what are you talking about?" That is why *Boy in da Corner* was what it was. It's the real reason why grime was accepted the first time. It was a very strong, detailed, powerful, meaningful album bruv and I listen to it some days.'

During the dispute – which has been waged in clubs on radio and on forums – over who started grime, it has long been upheld that Wiley was the original grime artist. But Wiley has since claimed it was Dizzee who began the movement. When asked in 2009 about being the 'Godfather of Grime', Wiley responded that 'I know it's a compliment, but why ain't Dizzee the Godfather? He was doing this before me.'

For his part, Dizzee claims the feud is more complicated than what's been said. And in spite of all the abusive things he's said about Wiley in various tracks he's recorded, in 2004 Dizzee said he wanted to take a mature attitude towards the feud: 'There's some deeper politics that the world don't need to hear. That's just bitching: "I don't like him because..." I wanna try and be as adult about it as possible.'

There's a big feeling amongst Wiley's fans and the media that Dizzee wouldn't be where he is today without Wiley. Dizzee dispels this myth by revealing that he feels Wiley gets way too much credit for having mentored him: 'I don't think Wiley was as important to me as a lot of people think. I met him from doing my own thing and I'd made a name for myself already. No one taught me how to make beats or how to MC. But it's not for me to sit here and slag someone off when I can't even tell you the way it was. That's a part of my past I'd like to get past, and not dwell on it.'

While it seems they still haven't made their peace, Wiley has said only positive things about Dizzee recently, regularly bigging him up and calling him his younger brother. For Dizzee, however, Wiley is still a controversial subject that   he doesn't want to talk about. To be fair to Dizzee it's been almost a decade since he worked with Wiley and understandably he's tired of having to discuss the situation in every interview.

The big question amongst grime fans is whether they'll ever reunite. The two have gone on to great things since their days hustling white labels and spitting lyrics on pirate radio. And grime and hip-hop fans the world over would love to see what the two artists could produce.

It would seem that, along with every other artist in the country, Wiley is keen to reunite with his old friend Dizzee. Stranger things have occurred in the music world, so optimists should watch this space...

18

MAKE SOME NOISE

In 2008 hip-hop and its place in British music was all that people were talking about. Largely because the biggest festival in the world, Glastonbury, had booked a hip-hop act, Jay-Z, to perform the headline slot. However, twelve months before the American rapper caused a stink with his controversial show on the hallowed Pyramid Stage at Glastonbury, Dizzee had already paved the way for black urban artists with his cameo appearance with the Arctic Monkeys for their main stage performance. In the summer of 2007, Dizzee showed Glastonbury organisers, Emily and Michael Eavis, that urban music had a place at the legendary festival with his collaborative performance of 'Temptation Greets You Like Your Naughty Friend', the 'Brianstorm' B side he appeared on earlier that year.

At one of the muddiest Glastonburys in memory, Dizzee and the Arctic Monkeys made musical history with their performance. In the middle of the track, Dizzee burst out onto the stage and began to rap furiously over the instrumentals in what seemed like a futuristic glimmer of how music might evolve if genres were allowed to collide and combine. The unique hip-hop/indie combination sent the soggy crowd into raptures of roaring and dancing. It was all put together quite last minute and Dizzee and the Arctics didn't have any time to practise the song. In an interview with *NME* afterwards, Dizzee explained it was not only the first time the band had played the track live, it was the first time they had performed the song together, as they'd recorded it separately in the studio. 'It was the first time we've done it live, we didn't rehearse, we just went on and did it. We'd never performed it before that moment.' Dizzee was really excited about the collaboration, exclaiming that the two acts created a truly special musical moment. 'It's musical genius, man! They did what they do, I do what I do, but when we work together it's basically a beautiful picture.' Dizzee has since become a major fixture at Glastonbury and other festivals, which he sees as a good thing. He told *NME* in an interview at Glastonbury that he likes reaching out to the wider audiences available at festivals. 'At festivals some people might be seeing you for the first time... You get to reach new people,' he explained.

For Dizzee, 2007 was spent climbing the musical ladder. In his tireless quest to reach the summit, he released two more singles from his third album. The previously discussed 'Pussy'ole' was the second single from *Maths + English*, released in July 2007, and it reached number 22 in the charts and topped the UK Indie Singles Chart for a week. Quite a feat considering it suffered from limited or edited airplay on the radio because of the 'offensive' chorus, which had to be removed. The B side of the single featured a track called 'My Life', on which Dizzee collaborated with an act from Dirtee Stank, Newham Generals. The single was praised for its humorous lyrics and ingenious sampling, and became one of the tracks of the summer.

A third single from the album, 'Flex', was released in November 2007. The track was a little dated, given that garage hadn't made any impact on the charts for at least three years, but it still charted at number 23 and spent two weeks at the top of the indie charts.

The video is set in one of Dizzee's dreams after he falls asleep while watching TV and is an amusing parody of the *X Factor* (Flex Factor). It features actor and DJ Reggie Yates as one of the three judges with Dizzee Rascal. His XL label mate, Mike Skinner, also appears as one of the performers, along with Peterborough United footballer Gabriel Zakuani and magician Dynamo. Instead of being a singing competition like the *X Factor*, the contestants, including Dizzee, have to dance for the judges. Two girls dressed in black end up winning. Each girl kisses Dizzee on both cheeks at the end of the video, before Dizzee, who's dressed like Simon Cowell, stands up from his seat, pulls his pants up and goes backstage with them.

September 2007 saw Dizzee head up the Mercury Prize nominations again. Against heavy competition such as Amy Winehouse, Bat for Lashes, Jamie T, Arctic Monkeys and New Young Pony Club, Dizzee was touted to win again, only at long odds of 33/1. The bookies proved right as he lost out to nu rave band the Klaxons with *Myths of the Near Future*.

The end of 2007 also saw Dizzee in another scuffle with the law, though thankfully in more innocent circumstances than on previous occasions. Having just passed his driving test Dizzee bought himself a Mini Cooper. Ironically, having just released the single, 'Sirens', he crashed his car into an unmarked police car in Purley. He recalled the story on Jonathan Ross, 'It was the first three days I had it. I was heartbroken. They [the police] were more heartbroken because they were written off. I drove off… This kind of thing only happens to me. My first crash; it's the police.'

Into a new year, and 2008 would be Dizzee's biggest year to date. He started off the year with his now annual tour of the States, followed up by the release of *Maths + English* over there – it had only been available on digital release up to that point. It was released on 29 April 2008 on the Definitive Jux label, and the US version of the album features new studio tracks 'G.H.E.T.T.O.' and 'Driving With Nowhere To Go', as well as a remix of the UGK-assisted 'Where's Da G's' by Def Jux label head El-P. It does not, however, contain the track 'Pussy'ole'.

To promote the album Dizzee embarked on a North American tour, where he performed with a variety of US artists. Fellow Def Jux artist El-P supported him, and Chicago spit-smiths Kidz in the Hall joined them for dates in New York and Philadelphia. LA-based Busdriver made an appearance for the Minneapolis date and Aesop Rock took the stage with Dizzee at Webster Hall in NYC and at the 1015 in San Francisco.

The US media largely praised the album and his live shows. *Rolling Stone* magazine described him as having 'delivered forty minutes of blistering, grimy hip-hop', while *Entertainment Weekly* called Dizzee 'an eclectic, break-dance-worthy Slick

Rick reincarnation'. Meanwhile, *Wired* magazine hailed him for his groundbreaking style: 'This U.K. rapper is the reason anyone knows "grime" is a music genre.'

Despite spending so much time trying to promote himself in the US and collaborating with US artists, Dizzee has always tried to keep a UK flavour in his music. Dizzee feels that people should have more faith in UK hip-hop and give it more of a chance, telling *Time Out*, 'People are almost embarrassed by UK hip hop and instead listen to so much American hip-hop that they say, "Don't compete, stay away from it." It's not a new thing: it happened to soul and reggae. People are almost embarrassed of themselves, when things are so close to home, coming from just down the road.'

Back in the UK, Dizzee released the track 'Dean'. Previously the B side on 'Sirens', it was put out to help raise money for Campaign Against Living Miserably (CALM) a charity that works specifically with young men in danger of suicide. The song was written in memory of a school friend, Dean Munroe, who at nineteen had thrown himself off a tower block in East London four years earlier, leaving behind a girlfriend and baby. Dizzee's career was just taking off at the time, but Dean's death affected him greatly. It's reported that three young men in Britain take their lives every day, and it was a message Dizzee wanted to get across and an issue he wanted to help with.

When Dizzee first heard about his friend's suicide, back in 2003, he says he was shocked. In 2008 he told *The Times,* 'It must have been super-rough for him to have killed himself. I still don't know quite what drove him to it. We have all been there, felt really low, back against the wall, as if the world is definitely against us.' Had he known how badly his friend was feeling, he says he'd have 'tried to ask him about what was going on'. Dizzee realises that men need to express themselves more, especially guys who've grown up on the estates and have been through a lot: 'They kind of feel that you need to hold shit in, suck it up, just firm it, get on with it. What a lot of young men don't realise is that if you've been through a lot of things you kind of need to talk. The more you bottle up, the more it'll beat you up.'

In the song Dizzee shows his thoughtful, vulnerable side: 'Death hits all of us one day, I wish I never had to hear your spirit run away…, Sometimes I hate this fucking world there ain't no denying it, 'Cos living life ain't easy but I'm still trying.'

The track was originally written as a straight tribute to Dean, but when he was offered the opportunity to help the charity he was more than happy to oblige. Speaking to MTV, Dizzee explained how he agreed to donate the track after being shocked by the statistics: 'I didn't realise that suicide was the second biggest killer of young men after road accidents. Before gun crime, knife crime, you know all the big things everyone's talking about now, people are harming themselves more.'

Dizzee wanted to raise awareness of a problem that's oddly gender-specific. In a ten-year period from 1996 to 2006, 13,718 men aged fifteen to thirty-five killed themselves as compared to 3,424 suicides by young women over the same period. Through MTV, Dizzee gave advice to vulnerable men: 'Find someone to talk to. You'd be surprised who can relate, who will listen, know what I mean? That's easier said than done, just try it at least.'

However, 2008 would involve more sorrow for Dizzee when his close friend, 23-year-old Kaya Bousquet, died in

February. The dancer, who had appeared in videos for Dizzee, The Streets, R. Kelly and Westlife, died in a high-speed crash on the M1 motorway. She and three friends, club promoter Patience Jackson, 22; singer Danielle Campbell, 23, and model Lyoni Ellington, 24, had been on their way back from seeing US R&B star Joe perform a concert in Birmingham when their Toyota Yaris was hit by a Parcelforce van on the hard shoulder of the M1. Patience Jackson was pronounced dead at the scene. Danielle Campbell died later in hospital and Kaya fell into a coma, dying twelve days later.

Kaya was a model, actor, club promoter and TV presenter from Marylebone in London. She starred in over fifty music videos and was a regular presenter of *Klub Life* and *H2O Honeyz* on Sky Digital Channel 372 and *Just Fabulous TV*.

With her beautiful (St Lucian, French and Jamaican) looks, Kaya modelled in glossy magazines such as *The Face* and *Touch*. She graced catwalks from London to Chicago and also appeared in numerous advertising campaigns and TV commercials, including Adidas, K-Swiss, KFC and McDonald's and is the current 'Ms Soft 'n' Beautiful'. Kaya was also a good actress and co-starred with Dizzee in the feature film *Rollin' with the Nines* and on her own in the TV series *Dubplate Drama* for Channel 4/MTV.

Kaya was more than just a pretty face, though. She was also really smart, with five A levels, and at the time of her death she was studying for a degree in Maths and Statistics at Queen Mary University. She also ran a successful club promotion business which earned her the moniker 'Queen of Clubz'. Kaya had organised parties for top artists such as Young Jeezy and Lethal B. She also knew a fair bit about music, writing a column for *Invincible* magazine. Kaya's sister Sequoia told reporters in the summer of 2008: 'Dizz was devastated by her death and has been to her grave with me since.'

19

TAKE ME TO THE TOP

In late 2007 Dizzee was having a party at his house, which was no unusual event. Snoop Dogg's *Doggystyle* album was blaring out of the speakers and Dizzee's house in Sevenoaks Way was bouncing to the vibe of people having a good time. The album played again and again and the party still kept going, and suddenly, like a thunderbolt, it dawned on Dizzee that he needed to make an album like this, one that people could party to. He recalled the moment of inspiration to *Clash Music*: 'I was having a little party at my house. Snoop Dogg's *Doggystyle* album had been on about five times, over and over. I was like, "Fucking hell, I need to make an album like this. An album you can put on and actually have a party." I wanted to make music that would make people get up, move and jump about, instead of stand around and want to fucking kill each other.'

Dizzee went into the studio with a whole new attitude. He was going to evolve from edgy social commentator to party-tune maker. For Dizzee the new direction was inspiring and thrilling. For his label, XL, the idea of Dizzee doing unashamed pop just wouldn't work. Dizzee explained the quandary to the *Daily Telegraph*: 'I said, "OK, you like to be thought of as edgy, I get that, but now the person who gave you the edgiest album you've ever put out is offering you a straight-up pop track. You haven't forced me to do this, I found my way there myself: you should be pleased."' The label bosses weren't interested, though. Dizzee had already fulfilled his three-album deal and was under no obligation to continue working with XL, so he left the label that launched him and put the album out on his own label, Dirtee Stank, telling the *Daily Telegraph* that he was quite happy with the arrangement: 'It was a blessing, though, because I got to do it myself.'

Free from his old label, where he'd been for five years, since the release of *Boy in da Corner* in 2003, Dizzee charged ahead with his new musical direction. The first single in Dizzee's new style was set for release in the summer of 2008 and was called 'Dance Wiv Me'. The track was Dizzee's first full-blown jump into the pop world and it involved a collaboration with electro-pop musician Calvin Harris and R&B singer Chrome. Jo Wiley made it a summer anthem a month before its official release when she made it her track of the week on her radio show at the start of June. In an interview with the, Dizzee explained that the *Edinburgh Festival Guide* collaboration with Calvin Harris came after they had met during Radio 1's Big Day Out the previous summer. Dizzee told Calvin that his record 'Acceptable In The 80s' had inspired him and that he would love to make a track with him. 'I think "Acceptable In The 80s" was fucking amazing. So when I got the chance to meet him, in Preston at the Big Day Out, I just approached him. We swapped numbers and it just went from there.'

Calvin Harris recalled the meeting on the press release for his album, *Ready for the Weekend*: 'Dizzee texted me, saying he'd done this a cappella over someone else's music, but his verse was too good for their music, so could he do it with me instead? So I spent a long time on it, to make sure it lived up to his expectations. I sent him the track, and he called me at two in the morning to say it was amazing, so I knew it was good.'

For many people the collaboration with Calvin Harris was a big surprise, but not for Dizzee, who feels that working with other artists has always been an integral part of his career, right from his early days: 'I've always been around people, always been collaborating. That's how I started off so that's always been my vision. When I did pirate radio I ran around with this crew and that crew; I wanted to be heard with that MC or that one. Not even so much out of love for them but more out of appreciation for what we're doing and out of respect for the art form.'

The lyrics for 'Dance Wiv Me' were written and recorded by Dizzee in the Dirtee Stank studio in South London, with extra vocals recorded by Chrome. Calvin Harris produced the music separately up in Scotland and later emailed the track to Dizzee for completion. Dizzee recalled in an interview with BBC's *Newsnight*, 'Me and Calvin met and we exchanged numbers. We never actually met once to actually make the tune, we did it back and forth over the phone. It was good, we were just like over the phone, "What about changing that hook a bit?" Chrome was the only one that came in the studio but it was good working with him because we've done a few things in the past.'

Before officially releasing the track, Dizzee had the small matter of playing the Park Stage at Glastonbury. Having impressed the previous year in his cameo with Arctic Monkeys, the organisers were keen to get the star on board. With Jay-Z headlining the festival there was very much a hip-hop theme to the event that year. There had been quite a media storm surrounding the announcement that Jay-Z was to headline, as Glastonbury is better known for inviting more traditional bands to headline the 150,000-capacity festival. The inclusion of Jay-Z attracted fierce criticism from Noel Gallagher, who said it was 'wrong' for Jay-Z to top the bill: 'If it ain't broke don't fix it. If you start to break it then people aren't going to go. I'm sorry, but Jay-Z? No chance. Glastonbury has a tradition of guitar music and even when they throw the odd curve ball in on a Sunday night you go 'Kylie Minogue?' I don't know about it. But I'm not having hip-hop at Glastonbury. It's wrong.'

Even Dizzee thought that having Jay-Z as a headliner was an odd call, telling the BBC, 'It's amazing to me, man, as a fan that's just like wow. I never saw that coming and I could never picture the Jay-Z at Glastonbury but it's all good.' When he was asked what appeal Jay-Z would have to an audience who are more into indie and rock acts, Dizzee said he wasn't sure about Jay-Z's multi-genre appeal: 'I don't know if Jay-Z has got that cross-over element. Kanye West or Eminem, they've both got that. Jay-Z is a bit of a funny one.'

Regardless of the fuss, Dizzee had his own show to worry about. Being used to playing to an indie crowd, though, he wasn't overly concerned. Bouncing onto the usually peaceful Park Stage to the sound of air-raid sirens, and flanked by two flaming pillars, Dizzee wowed the crowd with some of his earlier hits, such as 'I Luv U' and 'Jus' A Rascal'. Dizzee then launched into a mix of tracks from his first three albums, such as 'Where's Da G's', 'Stand Up Tall' and 'Sirens'. The crowd leaped around in the mud while Dizzee shouted out, 'Where's all my rowdy crew?', whipping the crowd into a frenzy of whooping and hollering. Dizzee ended the set with his new track 'Dance Wiv Me', with Calvin Harris, which prompted a flurry of manic dance moves in the field surrounding the stage. Later that night he performed an acoustic version of 'Dance Wiv Me' for the BBC, in which he announced that the single would be released the following Monday.

The upbeat party track went on sale on 30 June 2008 and instantly became that summer's soundtrack, going straight in at number one in the charts and staying there for four weeks. It became the twelfth biggest-selling single in the UK in 2008. The track also went to the top of the R&B charts, reached number 5 in Ireland, 13 in Australia, 40 in Belgium and 48 in Germany. It was, by far, Dizzee's biggest-selling single to date, going platinum in the UK and selling over 600,000 copies. Probably the greatest accolade Dizzee could receive about his new song was that he was the first British artist in fourteen years to go to the top of the charts having produced the track on their own label.

The music video for 'Dance Wiv Me' shows Dizzee and Chrome in a nightclub dancing, smiling and partying with girls, while Calvin Harris is the bar man. In the video Dizzee wears what he claims is the most expensive item he's ever bought, apart from his house, telling the *Guardian*, 'The reversible gold and black jacket I wore in the "Dance Wiv Me" video – there are only two of them in the world, and it cost a couple of grand.'

The tune's infectious rhythm spread like wild fire around London and there was no doubt that Dizzee's style had made the progression into catchy pop-tune territory. While most people loved it, there were obviously a few detractors, although even the biggest music snobs ended up loving it. Pop-averse *NME* admitted, 'There are many reasons to hate this. One: Calvin Harris, singing like he's reading the disclaimer on a direct debit mandate. Two: the middle-eight, where Dizzee tells his quarry she "made a real effort tonight and it shows". Three: the "in the club" video – more Slug & Lettuce Disco Tuesday than Miami with Usher. So just how is it so ace?'

With 'Dance Wiv Me' booming out of every speaker in the country, Dizzee had changed the face of UK music, once again. He had transformed from edgy, introspective musician to party anthem creator in what was nothing more than a flash of inspiration.

Just as Dizzee was changing the country's musical land-scape, another inspirational black man, Barack Obama, was changing the world's political landscape. As the world was marvelling at the dawning of a new age after the ground-breaking election of President Obama in November 2008, Dizzee was invited to speak on BBC programme *Newsnight* as a representative of young black Britain. He was invited on the show to give his opinion, as a young black person, on the implications of the election and the prospects for the British black community. It was a symbol of Dizzee being accepted as an icon and representative of his country, and a very proud moment that symbolised a level of acceptance he'd never received before.

The highlight for many was the comical moment when Jeremy Paxman addressed Dizzee in his trademark posh, aloof manner as 'Mr Rascal', asking, 'Mr Rascal, do you feel yourself to be British?' Clearly irked, Dizzee, who has expressed disdain for those British rappers who adopt an American accent and style, replied, 'Of course I'm British, man! You know me!... I think it don't matter what colour you are, it matters what colour your heart is.' Throughout the interview Dizzee was his jovial self, answering questions intelligently and honestly. He even raised the rarely addressed point that hip-hop music, and the backing it gave Obama, was a driving force behind the result: 'Hip-hop played a big part in this as well. I don't think he could have done it without hip-hop. Hip-hop is what encouraged the youth to, um, get involved in voting and making the place better and he is the first president to embrace it.' The legendary political interviewer was so impressed that he ended up suggesting the confident rapper should stand for office. Dizzee obviously took the idea on board and has since joked about running for office when he's been asked about politics, telling the *Independent*: 'Vote for me, man. I'm going to run for prime minister. I'd campaign for more strip clubs, better take-away food and no congestion charge in London.'

Dizzee also got to voice his views to Paxman on people power, when asked for his thoughts on political parties: 'Yeah, they exist. I believe in 'em... I don't know if it makes a differ-ence. But you know what I mean. It is what it is. Politicians... say what they say – you might get every now and again a genuine one, innit? But I think people, like, as a whole make the difference…'

Throughout the interview Dizzee maintained the suggestion that one of the main reasons Barack Obama won the election was that he'd found a way to connect with the hip-hop generation. It's a concept he doesn't see translating to this side of the Pond, as he told the *Observer* the following year: 'I gave up on the idea of politicians years ago. I know there is a negative and a positive side to that view. I will rap about injustice, document it, but I don't expect no politician to change it.'

Some people felt that Dizzee's boisterous manner and light-hearted attitude did a disservice to the black community, with other black artists like Craig David telling reporters, 'Dizzee could have been a little bit more intellectual with the responses… to a lot of people watching it fulfilled the stereotype of the hip-hop/grime MC attitude towards politics. I don't think that was a representation of black people in general, which the debate was about.' Perhaps he was referring to Dizzee's comical response to Paxman's suggestion that Dizzee run for Prime Minister: 'See, that's a very good idea. I might have to do that one day. Dizzee Rascal for prime minister, yeah! Wassappenin'.'

But Dizzee is never going to change who he is just because the environment might demand it: 'A lot of people wanted me to go on that show and act super-proper, like I'm grateful to be there,' Dizzee later told reporters. 'I was grateful, but in my own way. I'm not that guy in the suit, speaking the Queen's English. I don't need to be. I've done enough. I can go on *Newsnight* as me.'

For many people the whole incident may have been nothing more than a light-hearted joke, but for Dizzee it was a special moment, where he got some sincere points across. He recalled the interview to *Clash Music*: 'It was lovely,' recalled Dizzee. 'I went on there and got exactly what I wanted out of it. I think it went really well. I said everything that needed to be said. I said on there, "Yeah, Britain could have a black prime minister,"' he continues. 'But is the question, "Is a black man capable of running the country?" because sometimes it gets twisted what people really mean. There's two ways of looking at it.'

The singer Estelle – famous, at the time, for singing the chorus on Kanye West's 'American boy' – felt that the BBC presenter Jeremy Paxman was 'disrespectful' to Dizzee's sense of nationality. In an interview with the *New Statesmen*, Estelle said Paxman's questioning was 'out of line'. She said, 'Paxman's not going to get away with asking me do I think I'm British. That's disrespectful – you know, what do you think I am? I'd want to question him – and make him feel like an idiot.'

Estelle went on to say that it was particularly disrespectful for someone like Dizzee because of everything he had achieved to get where he was today. 'I felt so disappointed because Dizzee has come so far as an artist and a businessman that to go on there and represent us, represent all the musicians in the UK, it was like Oh. My. God.'

In a statement responding to the criticism aimed at Jeremy Paxman, the BBC said, 'Jeremy Paxman's question to Dizzee Rascal about whether he felt himself to be British was a direct response to the preceding comments from [the other interviewee] Baroness Amos who was saying that in the UK, as opposed to the US, we don't talk about the nature of Britishness and what it means to be British. The topics being discussed were race, nationality and identity and this question was a natural part of that discussion.'

The sight of Dizzee on prime-time television across the nation was a rude awakening to anyone unfamiliar with the star. Just as music heads had been jolted by the sound of Britain's youth when they first heard *Boy in da Corner*, so millions of British *Newsnight* viewers were given a sharp dose of British realism in the comfort of their living rooms. The *Newsnight* interview confirmed Dizzee's status as a household name. He was now more than a musician. He was a British icon.

Despite Dizzee moving away from his 'street image' and into the mould of a pop star, trouble still knocked at his door. Dizzee was arrested just months after speaking out against violent crime in the *Daily Mirror*, where he preached: 'The world is a big place and the more bullshit you do, the more time you are wasting. Think about life a bit more and know there is more out there for you. It's all there if you want it.' Despite these sound words of advice, it seemed Dizzee was unable to adhere to sensible behaviour himself when he was arrested in South-East London following an alleged incident involving a baseball bat.

On 13 December, BBC News reported that Dizzee was brought into the police after an alleged road-rage incident. Dizzee was taken to a South London police station and was held on suspicion of possessing an offensive weapon. He was later released on bail, before being cautioned. Dizzee hasn't spoken about the incident since, and it was one of the few low points in what was his most successful year to date.

In 2008, Dizzee broke free from the constraints of his record label, set up his own outfit and boosted his career further than anyone could have dreamed. He'd shown the music industry that he didn't need them and that, if anything, he was better off without them. 'XL didn't decide not to take me up for this album,' says Dizzee. 'I had an offer but it weren't the offer I wanted… They were offered "Dance Wiv Me", but they didn't get it. I put it out myself and it went to number one. It's turned out that I've done my biggest records on my own label. Of course it proves a point. It proves a big point. And it was the first independent number one in fourteen years, so it was an even bigger point… And then I did it again…'

20

STRICTLY VIP

At the start of 2009, there was no doubt who was the hottest musician in the UK. Dizzee revelled in his new-found pop super-stardom with a flurry of parties, diving head first into the champagne lifestyle his new sound promoted. It wasn't long before he started getting chased by paparazzi as he went in and out of London's hottest clubs. Going out, embracing the club scene and celebrating his success, Dizzee was regularly spotted around London, usually laden with drinks and surrounded by beautiful women. But Dizzee still loves nothing more than a good dance to some heavy music, and in London there's only one spot for that, he told *Giant Step*: 'There's a club called Fabric. I've got true players in that so I head there every end of the month… If I want to rave and sweat and actually have a good time, I go to Fabric… I get out here for a minute just to chill, talk, whatever, get drunk and I go right down to the base underneath the floor; it's fuckin' ridiculous the sound system in there.'

Unlike many A-list stars, Dizzee doesn't always head straight for the sanctuary of the VIP area either. He wants to get in the thick of the crowd and hit the dancefloor, and he's certainly not precious about being noticed. When asked whether people leave him alone, he replies, 'Naw, I get down, mosh. Strangers become my best friends quickly.'

But Dizzee doesn't want to just rave in London's superclubs. As he gets older, he sometimes feels like doing something a bit smarter. When he's looking to meet girls, drink some bubbly and be more refined, he'll go to 'places like Embassy... I like going to them places as well but that's a bit more [fancy]. Get some nice girls in there... dressed up, [getting] champagnes... that kinda shit.'

More awards would come his way in 2009 as 'Dance Wiv Me' won Best Dancefloor Filler at the *NME* Awards on 25 February. Dizzee picked up the most reader votes for his party track and the award ceremony saw him collect his prize from Brody Dalle – the former Distillers frontwoman, now with Spinnerette – who guest presented.

As Dizzee accepted the award, he thanked 'everyone who's supported this shit from the beginning' and bigged up Dirtee Stank's Newham Generals, who were celebrating with him on his table. To cap off the honour, he then did a dramatic stage-dive, award in hand, into the adoring crowd, to much rapturous applause.

There was no doubt that Dizzee was having the time of his life. And if his upbeat party lifestyle had been personified in his last hit, 'Dance Wiv Me', it was about to be caricatured with his next hit, 'Bonkers'.

Having spent large chunks of the previous twelve months in the recording studio, Dizzee was almost ready to unleash his all-new party-focused album in the summer of 2009 – but not before the release of his next summertime anthem. 'Bonkers' was released on 18 May 2009. The track debuted at number 1, marking Dizzee's second number-one single; third top-10 single and eleventh top-40 hit. The instant hit was a resounding success on the airwaves, going straight onto BBC Radio 1's A list, meaning it got the maximum amount of airtime. It was also selected as Jo Whiley's 'Pet Sound' and Sara Cox's 'Weekend Anthem'.

The track was another Rascal-inspired collaboration with house-music legend Armand Van Helden. Much like Dizzee, Van Helden has regularly been referred to as a 'musical magpie', sampling all sorts of genres to create his unique and uplifting party music. Like Dizzee, he holds no regard for musical segregation and is known for his love of rock and heavy metal, even though his genre couldn't be more different. On the face of it the two artists are from opposite ends of the musical spectrum, but if you analyse their careers obvious parallels become apparent, not least their prodigal pioneering attitude towards music.

Like Dizzee, Armand was from immigrant heritage, being born to a French-Lebanese mother and Dutch-Indonesian father who was serving in the US Air Force. Much of Van Helden's youth was spent moving around countries such as Holland, Turkey and Italy, which allows him to draw from a broad cosmopolitan background, while Dizzee – in his early days at least – took inspiration from the only thing he knew: the streets of London.

Armand has always been seen as the eclectic outsider of the house-music scene, much like Dizzee, who has often been ostracised from the grime scene for his diverse style. Neither Dizzee nor Armand are part of dance music's aristocracy, instead they're both musical alchemists who are at their happiest when holed up in a busy studio, surrounded by crates of vinyl, sample-hunting and looking to create the perfect beat.

Eventually settling in Boston as a teenager, Van Helden began his musical journey with the purchase of a drum machine, and it wasn't long before he started picking up DJ work around the city. He hooked up with US remix service, X-Mix, and caught the attention of US dance label, Strictly Rhythm.

Armand was a virtual unknown when he arrived at the label, but after a few years of knocking out some of the most banging US house records of the period, he became the scene's hottest property. This was largely thanks to a wealth of releases under act names such as Sultans of Swing, Banji Boys, Circle Children, Mole People, Da Mongoloids and Pirates of the Caribbean – not to mention a host of remixes.

To all intents and purposes Van Helden was still a label monkey at this stage. Everything would change, though, in 1994 when he ripped up the rule book and produced the club sensation 'New York Express' by Hardhead. This was Armand's 'I Luv U'. Tribal house had just began to make waves on the New York scene, and this track rode the pinnacle of the fad. Licensed by Englishman Pete Tong's FFRR, it became famous for its then groundbreaking slow-down, speed-up segment, the likes of which had rarely been used in dance music until that point.

In late 1994, Armand's label, Strictly Rhythm, dropped his infamous track 'Witch Doktor' on the world house scene. The song catapulted him into the spotlight and became an era-defining house-music track, played the world over, and for the rest of the nineties Armand continued to be the evolving cog in the house-music scene.

In 1996, Armand rocked the house world from Ibiza to Illinois, thanks to the impact of what was to become a truly legendary remix. His version of Tori Amos's 'Professional Widow' reached number one in the UK chart and has since gone down as one of the most infamous and epic house remixes of all time.

For Van Helden, the track turned him into a professional remixer for hire, and he went on to work on tracks for rock and pop royalty such as Janet Jackson, Puff Daddy and even The Rolling Stones. After this latest project he would be able to add Dizzee Rascal to that list. House music has never restricted itself with the same barriers as underground urban music, but still Dizzee appreciated Armand's ability to successfully genre-hop with extremely positive results.

Armand's crossover with Dizzee's traditional style – if there is such a thing – comes mostly from his drum-and-bass/jungle remixes. Just like Dizzee, drum and bass is one of Armand's great musical passions. His re-mastering of 'Sugar Is Sweeter' by CJ Bolland and 'Spin Spin Sugar' by Sneaker Pimps were both entirely unique in style and substance, and broke all conventionality with the associated genres, both house and jungle. Like Dizzee, Armand's music at the time was impossible to categorise and ridiculed by blinkered purists, but in hindsight his genre-less sound can now clearly be seen as one of the evolving links between drum and bass and UK garage. And with garage being the closest thing to Dizzee's early grime sound, there's an almost ancestral musical link between the pair. Van Helden has always fancied himself as the bad boy of the house scene. He's often talked highly of the hip-house moment of the late-eighties/early-nineties, such as Jungle Brothers rapping over Todd Terry beats, calling it a lost opportunity, which he was perhaps trying to readdress with 'Bonkers'.

Armand's genre of music was certainly seen as vastly different from Dizzee's, but the two shared a bond. Armand was one of the pioneers who pushed the boundaries of his musical environment, and unbeknown to the young Dylan Mills, this laid the foundations for Dizzee's musical direction almost a decade later.

Armand's risk-taking hadn't always been successful, though. Again, in a mirror image of Dizzee's career, he'd had issues with some of the major labels. Just as XL had problems with Dizzee's unpredictable style, the establishment had felt that Van Helden's scattergun approach to music was too varied, unpredictable and, ultimately, unmanageable. And just as Dizzee has a fearless attitude towards music, Armand's random approach has seen him flunk often. However, when it clicked, it really worked. The late nineties saw tracks like 'The Funk Phenomena', and its alter ego 'Ultrafunkula', dominate the dancefloors of the world. Further pop success came with chart-topping hit 'You Don't Know Me', with vocals by Duane Harden. With this track, Armand truly crossed the canyon dividing DJs and dance music producers from pop music icons.

While Dizzee was working the basics of music production in Langdon Park School at the start of the Millennium, Van Helden was becoming the globe's major chart-topping dance music producer. The past decade has seen him hit the charts regularly, as both artist – 'Koochy' and 'My My My' – and pop remixer – Britney's 'Toxic', Justin's 'SexyBack' and Sugababes' 'Hole In The Head'. He's also released a compelling and ever-varied mix CD – 'New York: A Mix Odyssey'.

His attitude of doing whatever he liked and not being constrained by musical genres has allowed Armand to carve out a unique position in the industry. Because of his unquestioned and far-reaching success he is in demand to work with anyone, in any field, he chooses. It's a path that Dizzee is clearly following himself.

It's clear that Armand saw his enigma-like qualities in Dizzee, which is probably why he pushed for the collaboration. Dizzee has admitted that he didn't listen to Armand growing up, being more immersed in the underground scene. However, once he heard that Armand wanted to work with him, he was on board immediately. In an interview for Australian TV at Aussie festival Big Day Out he recalls how 'Bonkers' happened. 'With Armand he kind of chose me. He sent me the beat out of nowhere. The name alone was enough for me.'

Armand lay down the majority of the track for Dizzee to rap over, and on it he does his hallmark trick of laying down a litany of booming beats, synth riffs and a rupturing bassline. And who could forget the moment just before the song erupts: 'BONKBONKBONKBONKBONKBONKBONKBONK'. Dizzee's lyrics ride the waves of bubbling beats perfectly as he seamlessly plays the role of an insane, claiming that a 'heavy bass line is my kind of silence'. For the first time, really, Dizzee takes another step down the pop route by going on a more repetitive tip with his catchy chorus. The tune was so addictive that it was stuck in everyone's head from the moment they heard it. There was still room for a testament to his roots, though, as he imitates Newham General's D Double E's signature vocal-warping on 'me' in the chorus line: 'There's nothing crazy about meeeeeeei'.

Dizzee uses a simple tack of having a single verse, eight lines long, repeated several times, plus the head-whirring chorus. The backing track merges banging house with an outrageous bass riff, not dissimilar to a heavy metal or grungy rhythm. It's another reminder of Dizzee's rock tendencies, reminding listeners of his love for Nirvana.

The track was an instant dancefloor-filler across Britain and the rest of Europe. At festivals around the world crowds would spasm and roar when Dizzee's gig inevitably came to a crescendo with his second summer anthem on the trot. For Armand Van Helden it was his second UK number one. But unlike Dizzee, who waited less than twelve months to repeat the mighty feat, it had been a decade since the house DJ had topped the charts with 'U Don't Know Me'.

Such immense levels of success were a surprise even for the ever-confident Dizzee. In the heady summer of 2009, as 'Bonkers' was playing at every party across the country, Dizzee told reporters he was 'amazed' by the track's success. After seeing the song go to the top of the UK charts he admitted he thought it was 'too gritty' to be a commercial success: 'Armand sent me the tune, I heard it, wrote to it. Then we sat on it for ages, didn't really play it out or anything and then the one time

I performed it live, it was bigger than 'Dance Wiv Me' at the time 'Dance Wiv Me' was number one. It's very, very dirty. A lot of people think I'm going towards the mainstream and that, but that is very gritty. It's almost amazing how it made it on to radio.'

By bringing out a second number one in a row, Dizzee proved that the previous summer's hit was no flash in the pan and that he intended to be a consistent presence at the top of the charts. For many the progression from edgy grime pioneer to mainstream superstar was completely out of the blue. One person who wasn't surprised, though, was Fraser McAlpine at the BBC, who said he'd seen the change as long ago as when 'Sirens' was released back in 2007: 'Ever since Dizzee released "Sirens" it's been obvious that his natural home is the top end of the singles chart – never mind the critical pats on the head and Mercury Prize nominations, never mind that other Dizzee tunes had been bigger hits, and he didn't really hit paydirt until "Dance Wiv Me" – something happened after he made that video where he's chased by fox-hunters, which changed his status from "top talent and spokeybloke for UK hip-hop" to "yikes! We've got ourselves a proper pop star here"'. As well as the UK, the track made it into the top 10 in Ireland, where it reached number three, and Belgium, where it peaked at number six. It was the fifteenth-highest selling single of 2009, selling in excess of 400,000 copies in the UK alone.

Armed with his brand-new number-one hit, Dizzee's stock had certainly risen for his third appearance at Glastonbury in as many years. After his set on the low-key Park Stage in 2008, he was promoted to the headline arena, the legendary Pyramid Stage – yet more confirmation of his mainstream status. Playing the 4.20p.m. slot, Dizzee marched on stage wearing dark shades, a pinstripe suit jacket and looking every inch the 'dapper don'. Within seconds, though, he'd ripped off the smart threads, revealing his classic baggy white T-shirt and jeans underneath.

Dizzee's set was a triumph. Now with more than a handful of well-known chart-topping tracks, he had a strong enough repertoire to carry the diverse crowd of 80,000-odd hippies, indie kids, families and ravers. According to reviews, his presence and charisma carried the performance more than anything: 'It was his personality that kept the crowd engaged during the set's quiet points, and his manner that spread enthusiasm throughout the crowd.' He had managed to draw a bigger audience than the previous night's headline act, Neil Young, and had the vast fields of people 'bouncing up and down in unison'.

The highlight, of course, was his just-released hit 'Bonkers'. As Van Helden's whipping base pulsated out over the sunny crowd, Dizzee hollered, 'We're going to have to get into "Bonkers" now,' as he head-banged and bounced up and down. The audience was treated to a real surprise when Dizzee's old friend and legendary crunk artist Bun B made an appearance on stage to perform 'Where's Da G's'. It was a real demonstration of Dizzee's international stature that a US star had come to the UK to play with a British rapper rather than the other way round.

Glastonbury 2009 will always be remembered for the passing of Michael Jackson, who died on the Thursday night before the festival kicked off. Tributes seeped into every single gig, from Jamie Cullum to Lily Allen, and Dizzee didn't disappoint, exclaiming, 'We lost a legend this week, so I think we should do something to remember him,' before DJ Semtex began a Michael Jackson medley with 'Thriller'. Dizzee later told the *Sun* how he was devastated at the King of Pop's passing: 'Michael had his problems but he was one of the biggest pop stars the world has seen. I couldn't believe it when I heard he was dead. I just sat and watched the news for two hours. Michael came up with some great pop tracks and I wanted to recognise that in my set.'

Dizzee branched out into yet new musical avenues during his performance when he covered the Ting Tings' 'That's not My Name' to open his show, before rapping over M.I.A.'s 'Paper Planes'. Dizzee covered the Ting Tings' number-one single, changing the lyrics to include several references to his record label Dirtee Stank and his grime past ('They call me Wiley…'). He'd also performed the cover on Radio 1's Live Lounge the year before.

Speaking to the BBC, Dizzee explained that he'd made up the lyrics when he was stuck in traffic: 'It was fun doing that Ting Tings' cover and it was nice to flip the lyrics. I was on the motorway stuck in traffic thinking of the lyrics I was going to switch up and change and I started learning them.' Dizzee also revealed that he hoped to work with the band, having met them at Glastonbury: 'I'd love to collaborate with the Ting Tings on a song. I met them at Glastonbury and I told them I was going to do this cover and I said, "We should work together as well and Franz Ferdinand."'

After the Ting Tings' opener Dizzee launched into old classics, 'Jus' A Rascal' and 'Stop Dat' before introducing new track 'Road Rage'. The middle of the set was filled with tracks from his first three albums before he picked up the party vibe with 'Flex' and peaked with 'Dance Wiv Me', next release, 'Holiday' and finally 'Bonkers'.

Everyone who saw the show claimed it was one of Glastonbury 2009's highlights. The *Guardian* gave the performance five stars claiming, 'The Dizzee Rascal knows what the mainstream pop kids want and he's giving it to them. Look out for his synthy future hit, "Holiday", premiered today.'

Even Glastonbury head honcho and cattle farmer, Michael Eavis, loved Dizzee, comparing him to the previous year's headliner, Jay-Z. Speaking at the festival press conference Eavis told reporters, 'Last year Jay-Z came, which turned out to be a hugely successful year and it brought all the younger people. We had a younger audience again this year because of what happened last year [and] because they thought this is a great place to be.' He added, 'They were all here in their thousands which was strange because the headliners weren't Jay-Z, but then there's Dizzee Rascal, fantastic! He's probably on a par with Jay-Z.'

For Dizzee it was one of his career highlights. A moment where he could see all his hard work being celebrated and enjoyed on the grandest scale possible. 'Glastonbury was amazing, that's the reason you get into it, man, the bigger the crowd the better,' Dizzee told *The List* a few months after the show. 'When you're doing things like Glastonbury main stage, and there's 80,000 people and your hits are going off, it's at those moments you sit back and breathe and take it in, man, 'cos it might never happen again.'

Dizzee was the toast of Glastonbury and had his second summer number one in the bag, but still he wanted more.

Calvin Harris produced his second summer anthem, 'Holiday', with chorus vocals by R&B singer Chrome. Calvin had originally written the song for girl group The Saturdays, but it was rejected. Dizzee and Calvin seem to have the Midas touch when they work together and Dizzee was keen to reunite on more stuff, telling BBC 6 Music, 'He [Calvin] produced the track. After "Dance Wiv Me" I thought it would definitely be good to work with this guy again so I asked him for another beat. He sent me a few and that was the one that stuck with me so I wrote a song. We left it for a little bit, this happened last year really, and then finally got it up to scratch now, everybody's loving it.'

The third track from the forthcoming album was released digitally on 24 August 2009, with a physical copy following on 31 August. Dizzee scored a hat-trick of number-one singles, with the track going straight in at the top of the charts, as well as marking his fourth top-10 hit and twelfth top-40 hit.

Dizzee went further into the realms of dance than ever before with this unashamed upbeat anthem. The frivolous video stars drum and bass legend Goldie and singer Chrome partying amongst bikini-clad beauties in a southern European villa. Just as the summer had begun with Dizzee at the top of the charts, so it ended with him there, too. Summer 2009 truly was Dizzee's summer.

It had been a crazy few months. He'd performed at Glastonbury, V Festival and Ibiza Rocks; he'd hung out with with Tom Hanks in Jonathan Ross's green room and even got to know Prince Harry backstage at the O2 Wireless Festival. When asked by *Wonderland* magazine which was the most surreal thing to have happened to him that year, he replied, 'It has to be Prince Harry. Tom Hanks is a real down-to-earth guy and we chatted about Snoop Dogg, because his son is a fan. But Prince Harry – that is proper royalty, man! We just had a bit of banter and that. It was mad. He was… a bit like me, really.'

21

LIVING LARGE 'N'
IN CHARGE

That summer's resounding success was followed up by Dizzee's hotly anticipated *Tongue n' Cheek*, which was released on 21 September 2009. As he'd been promising for the previous twelve months his new album was a fun-filled party album. As Dizzee told *Clash Music* just after the release: *Tongue n' Cheek* is basically a cheeky album, naughty but nice. It's still dealing with some naughty issues but it's on a party vibe fully, all up-tempo, upbeat and quite happy.'

The album opens with his signature tune, 'Bonkers', before launching into 'Road Rage', which, given Dizzee's recent alter-cation, was a light-hearted biographical moment. He embraces comedy in the song lyrics like never before and mimics the noises of the road like car horns. Dizzee goes on to recount a tale of going for a ride in his Mini Cooper just after passing his test, only to crash into an unmarked police car. The album goes into open-arms party mode with the familiar 'Dance Wiv Me' before getting racy with 'Freaky Freaky'. The Snoop Dogg-esque track comically regales us with tales of Dizzee's illustrious sexual conquests.

His old friend Shy FX makes another appearance in the ragga-infused 'Can't Tek No More.' Sampling Aswad's 'Warrior Charge' the track is amped up with jeep beats and sub bass. The song was inspired by Dizzee falling asleep at his cousin's house, only to be woken up by the MC chant of 'I can't tek no more of dat' from Franco Rosso's 1980 film *Babylon*, which was set in South London.

The album takes its foot off the gas with the more chilled 'Chillin Wiv Da Man Dem', a relaxed, almost blissfull, track aimed at smokers. Dizzee harks back to his chilled days of hanging out with his mates smoking weed, playing computer games and football. In 'Dirtee Cash' Dizzee tackles the current financial crisis. It's a reworking of the rave classic, The Adventures Of Stevie V's 'Dirty Cash (Money Talks)', which would later be released into the charts.

Dizzee gets as close to his grime roots as he's ever going to get in 'Money Money', but the subject matter couldn't be further from the impoverished days of *Boy in da Corner*, as he raps about his vastly improved relationships with traffic wardens and, of course, money, girls and cash. He even gives a brief nod to sensible spending and paying off his mortgage!

Dizzee relishes the control he has over his career in the head-bobbing 'Leisure' which brings in a bit of Dizzee's crunk roots blended with a funky synth groove. The album then culminates with the unashamedly boisterous 'Holiday'.

The album got great reviews across the board. *The Times* praised Dizzee for his sustainability, claiming, 'There's little elsewhere to suggest that Dizzee Rascal risks squandering the goodwill amassed to this point.' While the *Telegraph* commended the album for its fun, celebratory vibe: 'On *Tongue n' Cheek*, seven years later, he's in party mood, ready to celebrate the leisure society and its hedonistic culture of cash and consumerism. His pop-star status suggests that, now, the rest of the country wants to join him.'

The *Guardian* hailed the album for its wide appeal: 'It's irresistible in a way that would cause even a former adversary to put down his concrete post and succumb, in a way that even a dim posho who doesn't really like music would get.' The BBC, however, gave him the strongest praise, claiming that the album marked the promotion of Dizzee into musical aristocracy: 'A monstrously successful fourth album, *Tongue n' Cheek* is the release to officially crown Dizzee as UK dance/hip hop royalty. The boy's some prince, you know.'

Dizzee was definitely the hottest ticket in town. But when you're up on a pedestal, people will always throw stones, and accusations that he'd sold out came thick and fast from the envious underground. In *NME*'s review it introduces the new Dizzee as, 'Meet Dizzee Rascal, bona fide pop star.' Before going on to claim, 'Clearly, this is exactly the kind of pop star we need.'

Dizzee's progression from underground pioneer to multi-platinum pop-chart-topper caused a certain degree of controversy amongst the fans who'd been with him since the early days, but Dizzee remains unapologetic about his new upbeat direction. He has even suggested that it's been more of challenge to make his recent easily digestible tunes than the genre-defining sound of his early works. In an interview with the *Observer* he talks about his new-found commercialism, saying, 'I wanted to make some party music. I made hardcore music and that came kind of easy – it was what I knew. But it was a challenge for me to make a big pop tune.

Dizzee makes the valid point that, if he's to genuinely keep it real, he can only make music about what's around him. And at the moment he's not surrounded by the underground, he's surrounded by the commercial world. 'Parts of me are still the same person as back then, but I'm older and my situation's different. A lot of that is through travelling, doing festivals and trying to honestly reflect what I see in front of me,' he explained.

The world that surrounds and inspires Dizzee today is a far cry from the Crossways Estate in Bow that was his muse for *Boy in da Corner*. Back then, Dizzee was much more concerned with all the social ills and injustices that affected his adolescent world. The original angst-ridden Dizzee was concerned with day-to-day survival, teenage pregnancies and suicidal urges. Refreshingly, perhaps, *Tongue n' Cheek* finds him more preoccupied with the Congestion Charge, girls, dancing and champagne. Instead of having mic battles with the other MCs on the estate, he's now sparring with Jeremy Paxman on *Newsnight*.

While Dizzee's current persona shows a carefree, fun-loving popstar, his fans know, through his musical journey, that the new Dizzee is largely a chintzy front. He has bared his soul on previous albums, which gives him more depth than many popstars. In *Tongue n' Cheek* it's as if he's adopted an alter ego, as he tells the *Observer*, it's 'just the further adventures of Dizzee Rascal'.

Dizzee's audience is now broader than ever thanks to *Tongue n' Cheek*'s across-the-board appeal. And as he explained to Jonathan Ross, it's something that makes him very happy: 'I'm loving it. I'm loving that people are having fun because of what I'm doing. It's a lot more apparent, it's a lot more visible… I've crossed over to a lot more people. It might be your average young person coming up to me, I might get an old granny coming up to me now and that's wicked.'

Dizzee has moved away from the dense urban surroundings of East London to the leafy suburbs in Sevenoaks Way, Kent. 'It's quiet, it's cool,' Dizzee said in the *Observer*. 'It's still just about a London borough, I think,' which has prompted calls that he no longer represents the ghetto any more. His detractors just seem to be jealous of Dizzee's immense success. 'Ghetto people… I know exactly how to talk to them, exactly what to say. The way I see it everyone's looking for a bit of enlightenment, the more outlandish the better. But I want to keep it real with everyone, not just the guys on the estate.'

As far as Dizzee's concerned, 'selling out' is a vague concept. Was Michael Jackson a sell-out for making pop records, or Jay-Z, for example? In an interview with *The List*, Dizzee implies that 'selling out' is such an undefined, negative idea that it's not worth worrying about: 'No one can establish what selling out is. I can't be bothered about something which ain't clear, so fuck it.'

Dizzee's manager, Nick Cage, has pointed out that urban music in the UK moves at a rapid pace, suggesting that Dizzee gets slated for the innocent crime of trying to keep up and evolve. 'Things move so fast there that once you stop doing pirate radio and get into a studio then some people will think you have sold out.' But Dizzee is just keen on spreading his new positive message, while documenting the world around him. 'Uplift, enlightenment, a bit of social commentary, that's always been there,' he says. 'It's like if you work hard and really believe in your dream you can be whatever you want. I always try to get that in there somewhere.'

Dizzee's cautious not to let his new-found superstardom interfere with his career and his main goal of getting good music out to the people. 'I see all that celebrity stuff now as whatever, man,' he told *The List*. 'What's more important is that everyday people are liking my music, it's got to that stage. I've worked really hard for a long time for it to come to this point, where I'm putting smiles on people's faces, and I'm loving it.'

Now that Dizzee is so well-known, he's been touted as a 'role model' for how to make something out of your life from nothing. But Dizzee has been an example of how to make your life a positive force for quite a while, and it's a notion he's very comfortable with. 'I was a role model before the press and everyone picked up on me,' he says. 'People have been following me from when I was on pirate radio eight years ago.'

He is certainly a different character from the moody teenager who hustled his way around London's pirate radio scene. His success has seen to that. But Dizzee feels that while superficially he's changed, his core is still the same. 'A fundamental part of me is still the same, but I've adapted to every situation that's been thrown at me,' he says honestly. 'So in that way, I guess, I've changed quite a bit.'

One thing Dizzee's success has brought him is plenty of attention from the opposite sex, and he's rarely been short of exciting offers. There's constant speculation as to who he's dating and whether he'll settle down, but for the time being Dizzee's happy playing the field. As he told Jonathan Ross, 'I've been known to play about a bit.' Some day he would like to settle down and have a family, he admitted, telling Jonathan Ross, 'Eventually, I do, I want kids, I want all that.' But, the choice is sometimes too much. While Dizzee likes to fool around with lots of girls, he's trying to work out exactly what his type is – through plenty of research. 'I'm still trying to whittle down the kind of girls I'm into. Obviously I like black girls, I like white girls, but I like Mediterranean/Spanish looking, and I really like Middle Eastern girls right now as well.' So he's keeping his options open. When asked by Ross if there are any girls that he doesn't like, Dizzee replied, 'No not really.'

Dizzee has fallen in love on a few occasions but he isn't ready to settle down just yet, not while he's having so much fun. 'I've loved a few girls,' Dizzee said to the *Observer*. 'But then you get mixed up between love and lust, or I do anyway. But then every time I think I want to settle down a bit, I think… nah. There's too many…'

Dizzee has been associated with more than a few famous faces recently. He's been papped arm-in-arm with Natalie Imbruglia – apparently the pair struck up a friendship when they met on Richard Branson's private Caribbean island and have been seen on shopping dates since. Dizzee's spokesperson, however, denies that there is any relationship.

Dizzee is also reported to have chatted up Katherine

Jenkins at the 2009 GQ Men of the Year Awards, where Dizzee won Best Male Artist. At the awards show he also made fun of Kate Moss for storming through his post-show interview and grabbing all the attention. Kate barged back into the interview asking, 'Has anyone seen my lipstick?' Dizzee berated Kate with, 'You keeping stealing my light, man. Go away.'

Dizzee has also been linked, in the media, with Kelly Brook and *Big Brother* star Chanelle Hayes. However, if you believe everything you read, there are also reports that Dizzee's lothario reputation is not what he'd have us believe. In the summer of 2010 the *Sun* reported that he's had a secret girlfriend for two years. Perhaps he's kept her under wraps to shelter her from the media spotlight, or it could just be another tabloid fabrication, as Dizzee has claimed to be single for the past couple of years. He did let something slip in an interview with *Giant Step* in July 2010, though. When asked if he was in love he replied, 'Yeah, I would say that. Don't put that down.' He then backtracked, saying that 'I'm trying to keep up the single thing… I'm in love with myself, rather.'

Whether he settled down or not, his lyrics have referred to a very naughty history when it comes to women. But Dizzee has admitted to having some romantic moments, too. When asked by *Now* magazine what was the most romantic thing he'd ever done, Dizzee replied, 'I've done a few. I've swam in a waterfall in Puerto Rico, horse and carriage in Dominican Republic, jet skis, speed-boats on the ocean… Just doing some extreme shit, but lovely. Like movie star shit.'

A lot of Dizzee's womanising goes on at his after-show parties, which can get pretty wild, as he revealed to *TalkSport*: 'There's times when all that's going on: girls, champagne, this, that, hotel rooms, blow jobs, sex, banging, threesomes, all that. But there's times when it's just nothing and just bed.'

Celebrity certainly has its perks for Dizzee, especially when it comes to women, but for the most part it's something he struggles to get his head around. In an interview with grime blog *Blackdown* he explained how he felt about being famous: 'It's overwhelming sometimes because you're that far away. You have to check yourself, like "you serious?" Being famous… I can't fathom it myself really.' Dizzee admits that it can be annoying having to deal with the notoriety of celebrity, but overall he can see the positive side, such as the fact that people appreciate what he's doing. 'It does my head in, don't get it twisted. But you get over it, you know the people like your music and what you're doing. That's what it's about.'

Having spent the past ten years immersed in the music industry, Dizzee has seen a lot, especially in his early days. Back then he witnessed the rise and fall of acts like More Fire Crew and Pay As U Go. He appreciates that the partying side of success can become the sole purpose, which will ultimately ruin your act: 'I saw the whole Pay As U Go thing start and unfold and crumble,' recalls Dizzee. Same with the More Fire thing. When they were doing the first grime videos, I was about. I analyse. I'm always watching and I've always got my eye on the ball. And I've got a real genuine love for the music. It's easy to get caught up in all the extra shit. The money, the girls, the champagne… whatever. It's easy. I don't knock it but it's easy for it to become the sole purpose of why you do it.'

Seeing those two acts squander their talent, and having a few experiences of his own along the way, Dizzee feels he's learned some lessons about how to manage his career. These days he values the direct pleasure his music gives himself and others, and that helps keep him focused. 'I learnt a few hard lessons. Just appreciating things like crowd responses. Seeing how it affects people. I get a kick out of making people happy. Seeing people happy. Yeah man, genuine. I like getting paid but I like seeing 10,000 people jumping up and down, happy. 10,000 people who don't know each other necessarily, coming to the same place to jump around, to bubble to what you have, and forget all their bullshit for an hour or sumthin'. Forget all the bullshit in the world for an hour and bubble.'

Despite being an A-list celebrity and one of the country's favourite musicians, Dizzee still can't leave some elements of his past behind, and he has to be careful where he goes. 'I have to watch my back all the time. I'm a target and I always will be,' he told the *Daily Mirror*. 'There are grudges from back in the day that haven't gone away. A certain type of kid could see me and have issues.'

FIX UP

Rather than ruin Dizzee, it looks like success has improved him. Dizzee's new year's resolution for 2010 was to give up alcohol and drugs. Dizzee's new vice is his booming pop career and he's not going to let anything get in the way of his world domination. Dizzee told the *Independent* at the time, 'I'm not having any alcohol. No weed. I'm not doing anything – except some boxing to release energy.'

The martial arts are a big release for Dizzee. He's always been a big Bruce Lee fan, regularly claiming that he wants to master music in the way that Lee mastered the martial arts. 'He [Bruce Lee] is more than a martial artist,' Dizzee told *The Times*. 'He's a philosopher, a deep guy. I've been reading Lee's autobiography, *Artist of Life*, and there's a lot of insight into the soul, the world, life in general. It's not overly intellectual, but it's the kind of deep that people don't always feel comfortable going on about around other people.'

These days, with his partying behind him, he's keen to learn the ancient fighting techniques. 'I'm naturally slim so I like to bulk up a bit,' he explained to the *Daily Mail*. 'When I've actually got enough free time to do it, I like to work out four times a week. Everything from weights to the treadmill. I also do a form of martial arts called Jeet Kune Do, which relaxes me.'

At the start of 2010, things couldn't have been going any better for Dizzee. He'd just scored three number ones in a row, his album was selling well and the media adored him. Music magazines and supplements were full of chatter about Dizzee's pop dominance, culminating in the *Observer* calling him the defining musician of the decade: 'Like all the most pivotal musicians, Dizzee transcended genre. He documented the fears, loves, mishaps and misdemeanours of young Bow with an unsparing eye, in another league to all the MCs around him. Interviewed in the wake of Obama's election win, he made Jeremy Paxman look foolish on *Newsnight*. He wasn't scared of looking foolish either, pogoing in a shark costume in the video for his number-one hit, "Bonkers". He sounded like the decade: fast, vexed and funny.'

With his status sealed at home, Dizzee started 2010 with a tour of Australia and New Zealand. His album had sold well in that part of the world, creating a strong fanbase for him, and he played sell-out festivals of up to 40,000 revellers at a time. Down under, they couldn't get enough of him, with Dizzee being hailed as the highlight of the summer by everyone who saw him. For Dizzee, being big in Australia was a big deal and a sign of his global status.

Reports of a couple of minor fracas didn't overshadow what was a hugely successful tour for Dizzee, who revelled in his international popularity. 'The shows were easily one of the best experiences of my life as far as performing,' claims Dizzee. 'The people in general, Australians are wicked.'

Back in Britain his success was set to jump to another level at the Brit Awards, where he picked up the gong for Best British Male Solo Artist. The award was the icing on the cake after the success of *Tongue n' Cheek* and the greatest symbol of acceptance by the pop music industry. Dizzee turned up in a dapper tuxedo and performed a spine-tingling version of 'You've Got The Love' with Florence and the Machine, who won Best British Album for *Lungs*. Dizzee used the lyrics from his top-10 release, 'Dirtee Cash' (released the previous September) over the Source and Candi Staton cover (originally released in 1986). The performance was the highlight of the awards, with two of Britain's biggest artists at the time gracing the stage together. The track was released as a single the following day and went straight in at number two in the charts. The pair went on to perform the hit together at various gigs over the following months, including at each other's Glastonbury sets, turning the track into the anthem of Glastonbury 2010.

Dizzee spent much of spring 2010 performing with Lily Allen at venues around the UK before releasing the Dirtee Deluxe Edition of *Tongue n' Cheek*. To celebrate his latest album going platinum he re-released the album with an extra CD of some new material, remixes and live performances. It featured Dizzee's next number one single, 'Dirtee Disco', which was released on 23 May. Shooting straight to the number-one spot – again – the song features former One True Voice member Daniel Pearce and samples the 1972 Staple Singers' track

'I'll Take You There'. The hilarious video shows Dizzee and his accomplices enter what appears to be a local village dance organised by local priests. When Dizzee arrives the party really gets started. He is accompanied by a horde of hot girls who are much younger than the other dancers and all dressed for clubbing. The song and the video have of the feel of *Saturday Night Fever*, although Dizzee denies any Travolta influence, telling *NME*, 'There's no *Saturday Night Fever* influence. That's not John Travolta strutting, that's me, wearing a £2,000 Gucci suit. The moves are more influenced by *You Don't Mess With the Zohan*, Keep an eye out for the models – I chose them. The video's about being able to have a good time wherever you go, whether it's a club or a church hall.'

Once again Dizzee had the UK bubbling to one of his party tracks, and things looked set for another 'Dirtee Dizzee Summer' when he released the unofficial England World Cup anthem with *Gavin and Stacey*'s James Corden. 'Shout' contains extracts from the Tears for Fears song 'Shout' and 'No Diggity' by Blackstreet and was published by Simon Cowell's Syco Music.

Unsurprisingly, the track became another number one for Dizzee, beating competition from fellow grime MC Tinie Tempah and another World Cup song contender 'Wavin' Flag (The Celebration Mix)' by K'naan. 'Shout' sold well over 100,000 copies in its first week in the charts and all royalties went to Great Ormond Street Hospital. As many people said after England's miserable World Cup performance, you know you're in trouble when the song is better than the team.

Dizzee spent the rest of the summer on the UK festival circuit, putting in memorable performances across the country, riding the wave of pleasure his new sound was giving everyone.

September 2010 saw Dizzee feature on the English version of Shakira's song 'Loca', where he raps over Latin merengue music for the first time, proving once and for all that he can rap over anything. As Dizzee told gigwise, 'I know it sounds a bit mad now, but you'll see it and see what's going on,' he said. 'It's me doing something different man, on a merengue tip.' Dizzee was honoured to be chosen over an American rapper and is keen to move more into Latin music, telling *Billboard*, 'She's a bit of a trendsetter – she does loads of different things on a major scale.' He added, 'You'd expect her to use an American rapper [for the song], but she chose me. It meant a lot.' He continued, 'I'd like to be in that Spanish market. I got into the whole reggaeton thing when it came out, so I always wanted to get around to something like that.'

The track went number one worldwide, from Spain to the US to Colombia and Belgium. It was Dizzee's first real step into the global pop arena. Now that he's arrived, he's unlikely to the take a step back.

Looking to the future, Dizzee is being linked with every major British institution, from Simon Cowell to EastEnders. He has the entire country in the palm of his hand and people queuing up to work with him, but you get the feeling that the past decade was just the first phase in his career. For the coming decade, the ambitious musician will be looking at taking the next step. World domination. And at just twenty-five years old, who'd bet against him? As his ever-present manager Nick Cage says, 'He is established in the musical fabric now in this country. From that point he should be able to do what he likes.'